BECOME
UNSHAKEN

Joy,
Regardless

MICHAEL RODRIGUEZ

LUCIDBOOKS

*For my mom and dad, whose unconditional love and
dedication to hard work laid the foundation of my life.*

*For my wife, Stephanie—my constant partner on
every peak and in every valley.*

*For our six incredible children, my greatest joy and
my deepest why—my reason to rise, my reason to hope,
my reason to live with joy, regardless.*

TABLE OF CONTENTS

PREFACE

In the busyness of home, work, and the constant demands of modern life, I never imagined I'd have the time, or the strength, to launch another company and write a book. Yet here I am. As I sit in my home office and contemplate my next steps for what seems like the millionth time, a new sense of purpose rises in my heart.

Forty years of hardship, triumph, and learning have molded me into the man I am today. A man who deeply believes that real joy, lasting hope, and refined strength are not only possible but necessary for an Unshaken life.

I don't offer this to you from a tower of perfection. I offer it from the trenches of real life, from the mountaintops of victory and the valleys of despair, and from the experiences of heartbreak, pain, growth, love, leadership, and faith.

This is not a story about living perfectly. It's about living Unshaken.

Unshaken is more than just a concept. It is a vision. A vision to empower individuals to live a life Unshaken by the storms of life, to stand tall and strong in the face of adversity, and to find joy and hope in every circumstance. I carry this vision through everything I do and everything I strive to be. My mission is to provide a foundation for individuals to overcome life's obstacles, make bold choices, and live authentically—always moving forward, never looking back, and building a tribe that supports and uplifts.

The journey to becoming Unshaken is not easy. It's a practice and a daily commitment. And it's built on three core principles that I believe with all my heart can transform your life, just as it has transformed mine. It requires intentional choices, a positive mindset, and a commitment to growth. But it is worth it. Every step you take toward living an Unshaken life is a step toward freedom. Freedom from fear, freedom from self-doubt, and freedom from the pressures of the world around you.

As we move forward, remember that joy and hope are not just abstract concepts. They are the guiding forces that will carry you through life's challenges. Every day is an opportunity to choose joy, build hope, and create a life that is Unshaken. The obstacles you face are not roadblocks. They are steppingstones that will help you become stronger, wiser, and more resilient.

At Become Unshaken—a movement my wife and I cofounded to ignite hope and joy in people, regardless of life's hardships—we believe that no matter where you are on your life's journey, you are capable of greatness. Whether you are a teen, retired, or anything in between, we believe in your ability to rise above any circumstance and create a life that is full of purpose, fulfillment, and joy. So as you open this book and begin your journey toward an Unshaken life, remember this: You have the power to shape your life. You have the strength to overcome anything that stands in your way. And you have the ability to live Unshaken.

This is your time. Stand tall. Rise up. And live a life that is Unshaken.

Who I Am

I'm a forty-something-year-old man, born and raised in the suburbs of Chicago. Today, I'm blessed to be the husband of an incredible woman, Stephanie, and the proud leader of our blended family of six children ages six to fourteen.

I am a Christian, having recommitted my life in faith at the age of twenty-seven.

Professionally, I am an entrepreneur and restauranteur. I purchased my first Subway restaurant in the quick-service restaurant (QSR) space in 2011 after inheriting $41,000 from my father who had passed away. In thirteen years, I invested that $41,000 and turned it into a portfolio of twenty-five Subway locations throughout North Carolina that gross more than $10 million annually. And now I find myself the cofounder of Become Unshaken with my amazing wife, and I am the author of this message you're holding.

I am also a child of divorce. And I am a husband who has faced the pain of divorce.

My roots stretch deep and are diverse.

My life has been a journey to say the least, and on that journey, my life, family, friends, profession, and faith have all been part of what has led me to this mission.

My father was Puerto Rican and born in Chicago. He was a hard man, shaped by a hard life. But he was present, incredibly funny, and loved his children fiercely. My mother is Norwegian and the daughter of a potato and wheat farmer in Northern Minnesota and an elementary school teacher whose kindness fills every room she enters. My mother is a brilliant and accomplished woman—driven, successful, and fiercely strong-willed. She poured her strength and love into everything she did, but above all, she was a devoted mother who loved my brother and me more than anything in this world.

I come from a legacy of strength, grit, faith, and perseverance. Those qualities run through my veins, but they weren't just inherited; they were forged in fire. The fire of a father's violence, drug abuse, and alcoholism; the fire of jumping from women's shelter to women's shelter or disappearing on a whim and leaving our family home for good out of fear and self-preservation. Those qualities were forged in the fire of a decade-long struggle to keep a struggling business alive and the fires of divorce in the middle of the global pandemic. The truth is that life for me and many of you has been engulfed in fire. I am here to teach you how to find joy in it and through it.

Life is difficult. If you have ever come across another human being, you have most likely been exposed to difficulty. Sadness, anger, hate, fear, disappointment, strife, hopelessness, confusion, unsteadiness, and pain are all parts of life. They are difficult to accept yet inevitably guaranteed. I, too, have experienced all of these, as well as the many other difficult, painful, and tough times life has to offer. My journey has had peaks and valleys. A childhood of difficulty followed by a plethora of less-than-wise decisions and behaviors in life are what led me into adulthood.

A few years after college, I got into the restaurant industry, a profession that is unrelenting and ever-changing. Many of life's lessons I have been taught have come through this professional journey. God has used the hardships of my life and my career to teach me that the only way through despair is to have hope and to endure. The main point of Become Unshaken is to help each of our followers do the same. We aim to help each person navigate life's difficulties by using our principles in an effort to experience hope and joy in tough times. Nobody is born Unshaken. Each of us has our independent skills and natural inclinations. However, regardless of each person's natural individuality, I hope to build up each person to better endure and push forward. My goal for every person reading this book is that they find a way toward hope with the goal of finding joy while they endure.

I do not have a doctorate and I did not attend seminary. I believe it is for those reasons that I might find credibility with you, the reader. I am just a normal, everyday person doing my very best to survive, provide, and make it through the tough times this life and world throw my way. It is from my time in the valleys of life and my time overcoming them that I feel empowered to speak truth and hope to all. It is with a combination of creating strong values, defining and prioritizing your *why*, creating an Unshaken Mindset that is willing to both push forward and free yourself from your past that I believe you, too, can find hope and joy while enduring. Together, we can all become Unshaken. Thank you for your trust in taking this journey with me.

I am simply a man who has been beaten, broken, blessed, and rebuilt through the difficulties of life, learning lessons throughout. I am someone who has stared down hopelessness and lived to tell about it. I know what it's like to fight for my marriage, my business, and my dreams and still feel like I'm losing. I know the exhaustion, the doubt, and the nights where all I had left was a prayer that felt too small. We are not defined by our worst moments. We are not disqualified by our mistakes. You, too, can become Unshaken.

That's what this book is about. It's not about perfection, comfort, or ease. It won't give you empty motivation or sugarcoated promises. Instead, I will give you principles that are practical, values-based, and tested in the fires of real life. Before we get to those, though, we need to first understand the world we live in. The hunger for hope, the battle for joy, and the difference between fleeting happiness and eternal joy. Only when you know what you are fighting for can you truly live Unshaken.

Thank you for trusting me to walk alongside you. I promise you this: No matter how hard the journey gets, there is more hope ahead than you can imagine. I pray this is only the beginning of your positive transformation and purpose. Unshaken is more than a brand or a book; it's a battle cry. It's a reminder that while life is complicated, messy, and full of storms, we can live with hope, joy, and resilience.

Chapter 1

BURNING PLATFORM: THE STORM OF DESPAIR

The first draft of this book was like a college research paper—pages of stats and studies proving why we need a movement like Become Unshaken. But let's not pretend we don't already know it. You know it. I know it. Everywhere we look, whether it's the news, a scroll through social media, or just a conversation with the people around us, we see it. Hurt. Fear. Frustration. People who feel like they're barely holding on. Life can be brutal sometimes. It can feel unfair. And for far too many, it feels hopeless.

We don't really need numbers to prove that, but here's one that still makes me stop in my tracks: The average high schooler today reports more anxiety than psychiatric patients did in the 1950s. And it's not getting better. By early 2021, more than four in ten adults in America were reporting symptoms of anxiety or depression.

So yes, we all know the problem. Life is hard. And that's why I wrote this book—not to depress you with stats but to remind you that there's more to life than the pain you've felt, the hardships you've endured, and the unfair blows you've been dealt. There is hope. There is joy—not the kind that depends on your circumstances but a deeper joy that can't be stolen no matter how rough life gets. This book is my way of showing you how to hold onto that kind of joy and build a life so rooted and strong that even when the storms come, and they will, you won't be easily shaken.

If you're reading this and thinking, *I don't really need this message*, then good. I pray that means life has been kind to you. But for the rest of us who've been through heartbreak, loss, betrayal, or seasons that just feel too heavy to carry, this book is for you. The time is now to start your journey and Become Unshaken—to live with Joy, Regardless.

Chapter 2

HAPPINESS ISN'T THE GOAL

"I just want my kids to be happy." I hear it everywhere. At the grocery store, on social media, in conversations with friends and family. And I get it. It's a beautiful thing to want your children to be happy. Who doesn't want to see the ones they love experience smiles, laughter, and carefree living? But if I'm being honest—and I promise you I will always be honest on these pages—happiness alone isn't enough. It's not enough for our kids. It's not enough for us. And it was never meant to be.

You see, happiness is temporary. It's fleeting. It's a spark, not a bonfire. Happiness comes and goes based on circumstances. It depends on what's happening around us and, more often than not, what we are receiving from others. Imagine your child asking for a scoop of ice cream after dinner. If you say yes, they're happy. If you say no, disappointment suddenly rushes in like a flood. Their emotional state hinges entirely on your response. It sounds simple, even a little silly when we talk about ice cream. But the truth is, many of us as adults are living exactly the same way.

After a long day of work, if I walk into my house and find my wife has grilled up a 16-ounce ribeye steak, charred to perfection, I'm happy. What a blessing she is! But if I walk in and there's no steak, no grand meal waiting for me, should my mood crumble? Should I wallow in disappointment, questioning my worth or her love? Of course not. Yet many of us unknowingly tie our emotional well-being to whether or not life and the people in it give us what we expect. Happiness, at its core, is conditional. It is dependent on events, timing, and other people. And if you've lived for more than a few years on this earth, you know how unreliable all that can be.

People will mess up. They'll disappoint you. They'll forget you. They'll hurt you, not because they are evil, but because they are human. Even the best parents, the most loving spouses, or the most loyal friends will fall short sometimes. If our entire emotional stability is built on their ability to meet our needs perfectly, we are setting ourselves up for heartbreak.

That is why my heart aches when I hear someone say, "I just want my kids to be happy." Happiness, by its very nature, will leave them vulnerable. When we teach kids that the goal is to be happy, we inadvertently teach them that they must look to others—to experiences, to achievements, to recognition—for their sense of worth. And when those things inevitably fall short, they don't just lose happiness; they lose hope. They lose self-esteem. They lose the foundation they're trying to build their lives on. We were never meant to chase happiness. We were designed to pursue something far better, joy.

The Gift of Joy

Unlike happiness, joy is constant. Joy isn't dictated by the ups and downs of life. Joy doesn't leave when the steak isn't on the table. Joy isn't stolen when the diagnosis comes, when the friend betrays you, or when the dream crumbles. As Aristotle described it, joy is a sustained state of being. Joy is a deep, persistent assurance that regardless of what happens around you, something unshakable is happening inside of you. Joy comes from knowing that your worth isn't determined by people's opinions or life's circumstances. Joy allows you to be content even when life doesn't go your way. Contentment doesn't mean apathy. It doesn't mean you stop striving, dreaming, or grieving when necessary. It simply means that your soul is steady. It means your identity is not on the auction block being sold to the highest bidder of approval, achievement, or affection.

Joy frees us from the exhausting need for everyone and everything around us to be perfect. It releases us from the endless cycle of disappointment. And here's something you need to know: Joy doesn't mean you won't feel sadness, anger, frustration, fear, or pain. You will. You're human. Those emotions are real and important. But joy anchors you through them. Joy makes you

> *Joy frees us from the exhausting need for everyone and everything around us to be perfect.*

less easily offended. Joy helps you forgive more quickly. Joy gives you the strength to tackle a health diagnosis, a betrayal, or a failure with resilience instead of despair.

Stephanie, my beautiful and thoughtful wife, once asked me a question that thrust my mind into deep consideration as we began creating Become Unshaken. She asked, "Do you think people perceive you as joyful?" I had to stop and really think about it. Actually, I wasn't sure. I've always been serious. Intense. Focused. Demanding of myself and sometimes unfairly of others. For much of my life, I couldn't enjoy success because I was too busy criticizing myself. No matter what I achieved, there was always a louder voice whispering *not good enough*. I measured myself by comparison, by perfectionism, by impossible standards. And because I lived that way, I was unhappy—and I lacked joy.

But through real heart change and deep-soul healing, I have found joy. I have learned contentment. I have learned to quiet that critical voice not because life got easier, but because my foundation got stronger. Today, I am still serious. I am still passionate and driven. But underneath it all is a heart full of love, grace, patience, and peace. There is a deep joy that no missed steak, no lost business deal, and no failed expectation can take away. And friend, you can have that too. Remove the power that people and things have over you. Stop chasing happiness that will slip through your fingers the minute life gets hard. Instead, pursue joy. A self-sustaining, soul-rooted, purpose-driven existence that endures no matter what.

Life will test us. Storms of uncertainty, loss, and challenge will sweep through without warning, shaking even the most carefully built plans. Yet within each of us is the potential to stand firm and remain steady and hopeful no matter the winds. Unshaken is an invitation to build a foundation so strong and true that even in life's hardest moments, you will discover joy, hope, and strength rising from within. Over my own forty years, life has shaped, refined, and built three principles into my very being. They are principles that have allowed me to manage, endure, and even thrive through hardship. They are pillars that, when

Unshaken is an invitation to build a foundation so strong and true that even in life's hardest moments, you will discover joy, hope, and strength rising from within.

embraced, can provide you with unshakable peace and purpose, just as they did for me.

Here are the three principles I will share with you in this book:

1. *Comfortability in Silence*
   In a world crowded with noise and constant motion, there is deep power in choosing silence. It is in stillness that you begin to uncover your truest self—your real desires, hopes, and dreams. This quiet work of reflection is not passive; it is a bold step into self-discovery where clarity and hope are born. By becoming comfortable in silence, you give your soul room to breathe and your spirit space to soar.

2. *Define Your Purpose – Pursue, Prioritize, and Protect*
   Purpose is the compass that keeps us moving forward with intention. When you know your purpose—what truly matters to you—you gain the strength to prioritize it above all distractions. Your purpose is a light that doesn't dim, even when the path ahead is hard to see. Holding fast to your purpose fuels endurance and sparks joy, regardless of circumstances, reminding you that every step has meaning.

3. *Build Your Life on Unshaken Values*

True stability grows from deep roots. By anchoring yourself to timeless values—an unwavering work ethic, the grace of restraint and discipline, the wisdom of patience, and the determination to rise each day to meet life's challenges—you forge character that can withstand any storm. You live with an Unshaken Mindset. Those values not only shape your outer actions but also nurture an inner resilience, a quiet faith that whispers, *You are not alone, and there is always hope.*

With raw, vulnerable real-life stories; with practical, step-by-step guidance; with timeless principles as the foundation, we will begin to navigate the difficulties of life and build the foundation to remain Unshaken.

I promise you this: Throughout these pages, there will be nuggets of wisdom you can adopt, tweak, and make your own. This is your journey. Your life. Your chance to stop chasing temporary happiness and instead live joyfully.

Let's dive in.

Chapter 3

PERSPECTIVE – A MAJOR KEY TO JOY

I had just graduated from college and believed that all my professional dreams and goals were going to immediately come to fruition. It wasn't until the Chicago Police Department notified me of their hiring freeze that my imaginary belief that "the world is my oyster" began to crumble. I was a twenty-two-year-old kid in need of money to live my adult life. I had taken a social work job for a nonprofit that housed child wards of the state. For one reason or another, these twelve boys under the age of twenty had been taken from their homes and permanently placed in a group home. The kicker was that each of these children had a proclivity to violence and a form of mental retardation. These poor babies were the most neglected of the neglected. Most of them had been physically and sexually abused. The emotional and physical trauma combined with their cognitive challenges was staggering for me. They were physically grown children dealing with more abuse, neglect, and pain than I could ever imagine.

The job was brutal. I worked the overnight shift from 10:00 p.m. to 6:00 a.m. Any disturbances in the middle of the night fell to me and another social worker. Every night was taxing. And because the job was so painfully difficult and emotionally draining, the turnover was as bad as it is in the QSR industry. That meant there were days that my 10:00 p.m. to 6:00 a.m. shift became a 10:00 p.m. to 12:00 noon shift, only to leave and return that same evening. To watch those boys struggle with things like communication and self-care or to learn of the abuse they had undergone was heartbreaking. When I consider my own children, my heart weeps.

I will never forget the amount of work I put in with one of the youngest in that home. At first glance he seemed to be a completely "normal" child, just as you'd expect. But due to an unbelievable amount of abuse and neglect, he was left almost mute, hardly able to string multiple words together, and he was almost ten years old. I had volunteered to help with their Special Olympics basketball team, so I was working a double shift. I remember that he was in a better mood than normal and seemed to genuinely be enjoying himself. For a moment, it felt like he and I were having a normal day of simple fun and joy. That feeling of positivity and happiness stayed throughout the afternoon and evening. However, as I had come to learn and expect, those poor children were so unfamiliar with joy, happiness, and care that they seemed unable to accept it for too long before having an episode.

On this occasion, on a day I believed I had unlocked something positive in this young boy's life, he completely lost it. He became hyperemotional and began to aggressively attack others and himself. I pleaded with him to calm down and did all I could to reason with him, to remind him of our good day and try to use the trust I felt I had gained to level his emotions and get him to calm down. The reality? He was incapable of it. As he proceeded to try to attack another child, I was forced to restrain him in the most civil manner possible, according to our job description, yet the life in me was shattering. A little boy who deserved nothing his life had dealt him was stuck in a group home for boys with no ability or sense of love to support him. He had no skills to self-soothe or even the ability to use words to communicate. Fairness is make-believe. Life is not concerned with fair. Whether it is this little boy, the others in that home, or a child born with an incurable disease, they do not get to choose to whom they are born.

If you were not born with some undeserved, uncontrollable affliction, you should take joy in that. If you were not raised like these poor children were, then your circumstances are so much better. You see, perspective is paramount when enduring life's difficulties. We all know the term "living in a bubble." The safer and more unrealistic that bubble is, the more difficult your life will feel. It's why volunteering is so important. It is why experiencing the way others live is so important. It is why living outside of a bubble with people who do not look, think, behave, and act like you is paramount. Perspective is what helps us see our blessings.

> *Perspective is what helps us see our blessings.*

Please don't read this and think I'm saying that comparison is good or valuable. We should never judge a book by its cover, and what we see can't even begin to tell us anything about who a person is. But having true experience with the difficulties so many people live with does open our eyes to the realities of this world. If you were born in America, you have it better than 80 percent of the people in the world. If you have electricity, clean water at your disposal, and a hospital within twenty minutes of your home, you're better off than the majority of the world.

Perspective breeds joy, and a lack of it allows you to instead lament over things that actually may not be the worst things anyone has heard of or endured. To read about and witness the lasting, life-altering effects of these boys on a daily basis forever changed me. Does this mean that if my life and childhood wasn't as bad as theirs I don't get to be sad about things? Absolutely not. Does it mean that I don't get to acknowledge pain and suffering because I've heard about or witnessed someone else endure something that seems worse? Again, no way. Each of us has a right to mourn and lament our individual difficult circumstances. But opening your eyes and lives to others and their realities will also help you endure and overcome the hardships you are facing. Hope comes from perspective. And hope is what gives you the necessary strength and energy to push forward as you endure.

There is another story on perspective that I'd like to share with you. It was a moment that life—and more directly God—stepped in to both call me to action and receive perspective. I had recently been on the local news as a result of playing and winning on an episode of *Wheel of Fortune.* The experience was amazing, and I now have a go-to story for every dinner party for the rest of my life. At the time, I was a business owner who definitely could use the money, as well as the vacation that followed. I assumed that the reason I was blessed in this way was to help pay off some debt and take what felt like a much-deserved vacation throughout Europe. Life, however, had other plans.

Two weeks after my win made the news, I received a letter in the mail from someone in a North Carolina prison. It was sent to my restaurant that was being promoted on television. The name of the prison was stamped in bold letters across the top, and as I read it, my true purpose for winning seemed to become clear.

I opened the letter and read it. It was from a man who had been in prison for many years for a crime that just about anyone, including myself, would be uncomfortable with. This man first claimed his innocence and then made his ask. He needed support to transition from prison life back into the real world. He had written hundreds of letters to other people and organizations with few responses. As I read his heartfelt plea for help, I thought of multiple things in life that had taken place to prepare my heart for compassion toward this man. First, my father had been arrested many times and spent some time in prison. If my father—without drugs and alcohol—was a good and loving man and could end up in a place like that, who am I to judge anyone else?

One summer during college I also had the opportunity to work for my mother's social work company in Chicago. Working there gave me the opportunity to analyze and research gangs, gang mentality, and the entire justice system. I rode along with Chicago cops, sat in judges' chambers, and toured the Cook County jails. I realized that life is hard. To boot, I've always had a recurring nightmare where I am typically in a jail cell. Now, throw in the fact that this man who wrote the letter "felt told to reach out" to me, and there was no doubt about my next steps.

Over the next few months, the two of us wrote letters back and forth. He eventually admitted that he had a fear of judgment and rejection. One thing I needed him to understand was that I respected the justice system and that guilty or innocent, he had paid his dues to society. Eventually, I traveled to the prison to meet with him.

Think of every movie you've watched that has a scene of a prison visitation. Can you see it? I am here to tell you that nothing you've seen on TV equates to the reality of a prison. I parked in the guest parking lot with seven or eight other families. There were adults in their seventies and eighties and children under the age of five. We walked into a carport that was fence-encased and topped with barbed wire. Guards with shotguns awaited us and requested to understand our purpose for the visitation. My heart couldn't help but break as I watched loved ones in line enduring this reception as they went to see the ones they loved. Guilty or innocent, inside or visiting, everyone was in a prison.

I entered the prison with a forty-five- or sixty-minute visitation window, and I took that time to try to lift this man up and keep his trust in me strong. He was preparing to leave prison within the next month, and I was his only hope. The abuse, fear, and day-to-day life he had made me privy to over the few months of knowing him was petrifying. Eventually, I helped him find supportive housing and a job with the assistance of my church. This man would go on to go to school again and eventually got a job in a law office where he now seeks to prevent the same fate for others. He was able to prove that mistakes had been made in his case. He found both justice and peace. Today, he owns his own home and has a dog. However, years were unfairly taken from this man. Had a rough day? Imagine a rough decade in prison, falsely accused. Once again, my eyes were opened.

Seeing the real world firsthand allows for perspective. When drawn upon, that perspective can offer a mentality that is grateful. One of my pastors once made the statement to all those who believe they are self-made to consider where they'd be if they weren't born in the United States. What would have happened if they were born in the gutters of a third-world country with HIV? Would they be where they are today regardless? We have all been given something, some blessing that we've utilized to get us where we are and allow us the opportunities to go where we want to go.

That does not mean that hardship does not make things more difficult. It doesn't mean that if you didn't have the same difficult trials I've mentioned that your life is easy and that there are no explanations, reasons, or excuses that achieving a joy-filled life is difficult. But recognizing the realities that so many people in the world experience does transform your heart. That heart change and realistic perspective on what my life could have been does help me realize the blessings I do have. A healthy brain that works as it should. Being born in the greatest, most democratic, free society of opportunity on the planet. Having two parents who love me despite their human shortcomings. Having six healthy children and a supportive wife.

Often, I believe that we as humans, and especially Americans, believe that this is the starting point—that these types of blessings are a right that all should have. I am here to tell you that is a fallacy. The world and every person in it are broken. I avoid adages and cliches, but this one is simply a fact. It can always be worse. The fact that it isn't worse is a blessing. A blessing that should bring you joy. Allow that perspective to generate joy in your heart and life today. Be thankful. Bask in it. Life is good.

One of the greatest gifts we can give ourselves both personally and professionally is the pursuit of a diversity of experience. Engaging with people from different walks of life, stepping into environments far outside our comfort zones, and allowing ourselves to see the world through lenses other than our own build a depth of understanding that can't be gained any other way. I've been profoundly shaped by experiences that exposed me to the lives of the imprisoned and the abused. Stories of struggle and hardship far beyond my own. Those encounters gave me something invaluable: perspective. They reminded me again and again to put my own difficulties in context, stay grounded in gratitude, and recognize the incredible resilience of the human spirit. When we open ourselves to these kinds of experiences, we stretch our capacity for empathy, compassion, and humility, and that strengthens us to remain Unshaken in our own trials.

This diversity of experience is becoming even more essential in today's world. In many ways, our society has grown increasingly isolated, especially in the wake of COVID. Remote work, at-home learning, and an ever-deepening reliance on technology have at times shrunk our circles and dulled our human connections. Yet there's hope in knowing that we have the power to push back against that trend. By intentionally seeking out relationships, stories, and experiences that differ from our own, we not only enrich our understanding but also build stronger foundations for joy, resilience, and clarity of purpose. It's a reminder that even when life feels smaller or more confined, our perspectives—and the strength they give us—can keep expanding. And in that growth, we find a deeper steadiness, a firmer footing, and a renewed sense of joy that is anything but shaken.

Restoring the Foundation – Finding Stability After Divorce

As we've explored so far, life has a way of testing the foundations we stand on, shaking us in ways we never expected. Before we move into the core Unshaken principles and values, I want to share a personal story that shaped my understanding of what it truly means to stand firm in who you are, even when everything around you feels uncertain. This story isn't just a memory; it's a moment that marked a turning point, refining my perspective and deepening my convictions. As you read, I invite you to reflect on your own journey and prepare your heart for the practical truths that follow.

There are chapters in life that we don't speak of easily, not because we carry shame but because the layers are too complex to unpack quickly. Divorce is one of those chapters. For me, it wasn't a moment. It was a season, a long, exhausting stretch of emotional and spiritual fatigue that forced me to examine what it means to truly live out the values I claimed to believe.

At one point on that journey, my sense of identity began to fade. My confidence, peace, and internal compass felt clouded. I was doing everything I could to stay the course and protect what mattered most to me—my family, my integrity, and my faith. And yet despite all my efforts, I found myself living in a reality that no longer aligned with who I knew I was or who I was called to be.

The foundation I had built over decades, perseverance, patience, and faith, was under strain, not by one moment or one decision but by a growing recognition that something was breaking down in ways I couldn't fix with willpower alone. It's a strange thing to feel isolated while living in a full house and even harder when you don't fully understand how or when the shift occurred.

Over time, I had to wrestle with one of the hardest truths of all—that for me, staying the same wasn't strength. It was slowly becoming survival. I didn't come to that realization quickly or carelessly. It was the result of prayer, counsel, silence, and a long internal battle to discern what health and wholeness would truly require.

Choosing to end that chapter didn't erase the pain. It didn't solve every struggle. In fact, some new ones emerged, particularly the ache of not being with my children every day. That grief, for any parent who's walked it, is real. And yet even in that loss, something new was born. I became intentional in a way I never had to be before. Every moment, every conversation, and every embrace took on deeper meaning.

I had to rebuild, not just a life but a mindset. I had to anchor again to the Unshaken values that had always guided me, but this time it was from a place of brokenness. In that season, I learned that hardship doesn't always destroy us. It reveals the parts of us we've neglected, the parts that still have strength we forgot we carried.

This story is not about blame or bitterness. It's about reclaiming. It's about rediscovering who you are when life unravels and choosing deliberately to rise again. I didn't walk out of that season untouched, but I walked out refined. Stronger. Clearer. Grateful. I share this not to open old wounds but to offer solidarity. If you're walking through your own storm—divorce, loss, identity crisis, emotional collapse—let this be a quiet reminder that you are not done. You can rebuild. You can protect what matters most. You can rediscover the strength that still lives inside you. Sometimes the greatest act of courage isn't holding on; it's knowing when it's time to begin again.

In the aftermath of that season, I stood in the rubble, but also in a strange kind of freedom. It was as if life handed me a blank canvas, asking not who I had been but who I would choose to become. I began the slow process of remembering and relearning who I truly was, not the version shaped by pain but the one grounded in purpose, character, and conviction.

I returned to what mattered most: my faith, my family, my children, and the calling to live a life marked by steadiness and strength. In that quiet rebuilding, I anchored into the values that had always been in me, though momentarily buried: integrity, peace, and joy that flows from alignment, not circumstances. I remembered and rebuilt on my foundation of faith and the principles that define Unshaken—hard work, patience, discipline, and the strength to rise, even when it hurts. I had rebuilt and anchored into my Unshaken Mindset.

Those weren't just ideals; they were battle-tested truths. It was a painful, soul-deep rebuilding. It took years. Years of remembering who I was before life's erosion began. Years of anchoring into the principles that had once defined me and choosing daily to live by them again.

Those are the truths I now share in this book. Not ideas, but realities I had to fight for, proven ways to endure with both hope and joy, even when life falls apart. I wrestled to find my footing again in the silence that followed divorce and the stillness COVID unexpectedly created. It was a season of confronting pain with humility, not bitterness or blame, and finding a way forward with resolve. In that struggle, Unshaken was lived out one day, one decision, and one act of courage at a time.

Joy is not the absence of struggle. It is the presence of something deeper that remains even when everything else is shaking. And perspective is what sharpens our vision to see it. The goal of Unshaken is not to offer platitudes or polished clichés but to hold space for the real, raw, and redemptive moments of life and show that joy is still possible regardless. And it's not because life gets easier; it's because we become

> *Joy becomes our resistance, our testimony, and ultimately our inheritance.*

stronger. We anchor deeper. Joy becomes our resistance, our testimony, and ultimately our inheritance.

What comes next are not theories but lived truths. Principles born from fire, tested in silence, and refined in the tension between hope and heartbreak. These values are not presented as formulas for perfection but as guides for stability. Anchors for the soul when everything around you feels unstable.

As we turn the page from pain to purpose, the next section of this book will explore the foundational principles of

Unshaken—what they are, why they matter, and how they can ground you in the kind of joy that endures.

This is the shift from surviving to building, from holding on to rising up. The storm may have shaken everything, but now it's time to rebuild on what cannot be moved.

Throughout the sections that follow, you'll find:

- *A Story (or Two):* A life experience where this principle became real for me.
- *Practical Steps:* Clear, actionable advice to begin implementing the principle in your own life.

I didn't learn these principles because I was strong. I learned them because I was struggling, and strength still showed up. And I believe it can show up for you too.

Chapter 4

PRINCIPLE 1: COMFORTABILITY WITH SILENCE – MEETING YOUR TRUE SELF

The modern world hates silence. Yet it is in silence that we meet our true selves—our deepest desires, fears, aspirations, and dreams. It is in the quiet moments, the stillness among the chaos, that we can hear what our hearts are actually whispering. It is in silence that we stop reacting and start understanding. The truth is that silence forces us to confront ourselves. It strips away distraction and demands honesty. And that can be terrifying if we're not prepared. But it can also be liberating, because when you get comfortable with silence, you learn two critical things: what you are truly longing for and what has been standing in your way.

> *But it can also be liberating, because when you get comfortable with silence, you learn two critical things: what you are truly longing for and what has been standing in your way.*

Without the crutch of external noise, your soul finally gets a voice. And if you listen carefully, it will start to tell you what it truly desires. Not what culture says you should want, not what your parents expected from you, not even what you've been pretending you care about just to fit in. It's in silence that your real dreams start to emerge.

In 2014, a study titled "Just Think: The Challenges of the Disengaged Mind" was conducted by psychologists Timothy D. Wilson and his colleagues from the University of Virginia and Harvard University. It was published in the journal *Science* in July 2014. The researchers conducted eleven experiments involving over 700 participants. In those studies, individuals were asked to sit alone in a room without any distractions—no phones, books, or other stimuli—for periods ranging from six to fifteen minutes. They were instructed to entertain themselves solely with their thoughts.

The findings revealed that many participants found the experience unpleasant. In one notable experiment, participants were given the option to self-administer a mild electric shock during the thinking period. Despite previously stating they would pay to avoid such a shock, 67 percent of men and 25 percent of women chose to shock themselves at least once during the fifteen-minute session. One male participant administered 190 shocks to himself.

The study suggests that many people prefer engaging in some activity, even an unpleasant one, over being alone with their thoughts. Where would you fall in this experiment? Would you choose to administer an electric shock to yourself as opposed to sitting in silence for no more than fifteen minutes?

The researchers proposed that the human mind may struggle to focus on pleasant thoughts and is prone to wandering into negative or ruminative patterns when undirected. They indicated that this discomfort with introspection might explain the widespread reliance on constant external stimulation in modern life.

These findings highlight the challenges of disengaging from external stimuli and the potential benefits of practices like mindfulness and meditation to help individuals become more comfortable with their internal experiences. It also shows that if we have trained our minds to require constant stimulation or have become so used to distraction that our brains now struggle to be both calm and positive, some serious retraining is necessary. Since I believe this information is true, let me dive into my own need and experience with this retraining and recentering of my mind and life.

The world and the enemy of joy is loudness. Consider your day today. You were awakened by an alarm that alerted you to jump out of bed and get your day started. My alarm, much to my wife's chagrin, sounds like a submarine that has just been hit by a torpedo. When that alarm goes off, there is no choice but to get out of bed. We both run to the bathroom to quickly freshen up before getting all six of our children out of bed, each requiring a separate style of wakening. Some require back rubs and "sweethearts." Others won't move without the shock of a ceiling light and the threat of missing breakfast. Cue the making of lunches, brushing of hair and teeth, and the battle is on against a clock that moves in ten-minute increments, not sixty seconds.

Now the car is loaded and we are off. Some want music, and others want to talk about the day ahead. Carpooling at multiple schools always takes longer than expected, and now we are somehow eighteen minutes behind schedule. We have only been up for one hour. My phone starts dinging with issues my store openers have walked into, and my wife is already on her fourth email. And it isn't even 8:30 a.m. From there, only chaos ensues until our 8:30 p.m. and 9:00 p.m. bedtime routines are complete. From there we have a choice: shower and bed, Netflix binge, or sit and connect.

Let me be clear. I love absolutely everything I've just described. I am able to find joy in the busyness because it is done with the *whys* of my life. But there is zero chill in our day. This fall we have twenty-four practices or games every week to get our kids to. I coach at least half of those teams every season of the year. I have many friends and acquaintances who have similar lives, responsibilities, and schedules. We are all exhausted. Routinely my wife and I find ourselves being asked, "How do you do it?" Yes, six kids are a ton. Owning twenty-five restaurants shows I am a glutton for pain and difficulty. And my wife is a senior human resource professional at a Fortune 500 company. We raise our own children, clean our own home, divide and conquer to attend every game, and remain present for both our children and each other. We are still able to show up with smiles on our hearts, joyful in the chaos and difficulty. Let me speak to how I was able to get there.

When I graduated from high school and entered my freshman year at the University of Illinois Urbana-Champaign, I wasn't entirely sure what I wanted to "be when I grew up." I had done little research on professions and had very little exposure outside of the adults in my life and their own careers. As a result, I had settled on becoming a lawyer, most likely because one of my mom's favorite shows was *Law and Order*. A lawyer was my fallback once I realized I wasn't going to play in the NBA. I had zero legitimate direction and knew very little about myself or my options at the age of eighteen. So there I was, unsure of my direction and without a goal of value to me.

The summer before I entered college I stumbled upon a singing competition and somehow won an opportunity to try out for Jive Records. The tryout, which was a few months after college began, ended with an opportunity, or a "carrot" so to speak. I could drop out of college and move to Los Angeles for a chance to be signed, or I could continue on the path I was on outside of music. I had no desire to become a poor, grind-it-out musician, and my freshman year so far was already more fun than I could have imagined, so my decision was easy. But I made that decision because I had no direction in any way. College was more fun, so I chose it over music. It was a decision made on a whim and made selfishly. What did I want in that very moment? I had no consideration of my aspirations or future. I was living in the here and now.

Fast forward to graduation. I had skipped the lawyer career path and decided to get into law enforcement. I applied to the Chicago Police Department, the FBI, the CIA, and the U.S. Department of Energy. I chose law enforcement because I believed that being a lawyer wasn't in fact what I wanted. I wanted to be in trials, tripping up criminals and talking my way through court cases for an intrigued jury. What I learned was that most of my time would be spent with a red pen and thousands of pages of documents. Again, I was still unsure of who I was, what I wanted out of life, and what my purpose was. At twenty-two, I had yet to learn the most important thing about myself. Who was I, and what drove me as a human being?

As I waited to be hired by some law enforcement agency, I got jobs in social work. They taught me many things about the world and coincidentally led me to get the perspectives on life that I still carry to this day. But in the moment, I did not appreciate them for what they became to me later in life.

Fast forward again if you will to March 2020, and my then-wife and I made the decision that a divorce was the best way to move forward as happy, healthy parents for the sake of our children. That decision was not made lightly but was also very clearly the correct decision for us both. The decision we made led us right into the global COVID pandemic. We agreed to split the family up as the world was shutting down. My family of six suddenly became a family of one half of the time. Throw in the fear of being a business owner who had just purchased two locations six months before, and I saw the financial strain of a divorce and the debt of my business piling up. To boot, I was now alone in my four-bedroom home with nothing but myself and the ticking of a wall clock.

Don't get me wrong, this time was very much utilized to catch up on five years of television. I watched every culturally significant show that had been created over the previous eight years. When I was a business owner and full-time daddy, I couldn't watch shows like *Game of Thrones* and *Schitt's Creek*. Thankfully, COVID also blessed me with the chance to make up for those lost times. But I digress. The underlying feeling in those initial months was loneliness. The feelings of solitude and the absence of children's laughter and wrestling were deafening. My world was upside down, and my future for the first time in years was completely unknown. All I had for most of my days was me, myself, and I.

After the mourning of an ended marriage and the pain of not having my children with me every moment, I began to accept it more easily. I was able to shift my mindset. The silence in those moments stopped scaring me and instead became a transformational opportunity. I had a choice to make. I could allow the silence, solitude, and loneliness to consume me, or I could use it as a tool.

The silence and removal of distraction allowed me to deep dive into myself. Who was I? What did I want in life? What did I want the lives of my children to look like? I was able to reevaluate decisions I had made in the past, assess mistakes and missteps, and then build myself up in ways to prevent a repeat performance. Our fear of loneliness and silence is what leads us to make poor and irrational decisions. We must learn to appreciate ourselves and comfort ourselves to avoid making rash, fearful choices. Taking time to become comfortable in silence and learning to listen to your own voice over others can help transform and grow self-love.

Looking back, I can clearly see how two powerful forces shaped the most transformative season of my life. Those forces were diving deep into my faith and consistently taking advantage of therapy. Together, they helped me peel back the layers of who I thought I was so I could discover who I was truly created to be. It was in the space between Scripture and silence, reflection and conversation that I found healing. That healing helped prepare me for what would become the most joyful, purpose-driven, and fruitful chapter of my life.

> *That healing helped prepare me for what would become the most joyful, purpose-driven, and fruitful chapter of my life.*

Therapy has been part of my journey for a long time. Thanks to my mom, I was first introduced to it as a child after I went through some early experiences that left me angry and emotionally raw. That initial exposure planted a seed. Later, after college, I returned to therapy, this time to cope with the depression I felt when life didn't seem to be lining up with the dreams I had imagined. Those early seasons, though brief, helped normalize the idea of therapy for me. And that would make all the difference years later when I would need it the most.

Just before the COVID-19 pandemic, I had begun therapy sessions, this time trying to navigate the demands of marriage, fatherhood, and the relentless pressure of running a business. The timing was divine. When everything in the world began to unravel, I already had an anchor. My therapist became a steady voice in a storm. He was compassionate, insightful, and unflinchingly committed to helping me understand myself. And this time, therapy wasn't just about talking; it was about transforming.

With my therapist's help, I started to unpack deeply buried emotions—shame, confusion, self-doubt, disappointment. I traced their origins, confronted the false narratives I had unknowingly accepted, and began replacing them with truths rooted in love, clarity, and grace. It was like being reintroduced to myself, not just the person I had been but the person I could become. Therapy became a mirror, a lifeline, and a compass all at once.

I say this often: Your mental and emotional health cannot be ignored. It's just as essential as a good diet, consistent exercise, or a financial strategy. Therapy gave me space to understand who I am, what I value, and what I truly want out of life. And that clarity leads to purpose. It's when we lack self-awareness—when we don't pause to truly know ourselves—that we start chasing someone else's version of success, mistaking their dream for ours. But joy doesn't live there. You can't find peace pursuing a path that was never yours to begin with.

> *You can't find peace pursuing a path that was never yours to begin with.*

Therapy helped give me that space to reflect, dream honestly, and let go of what was never meant for me. In the midst of a world drowning in anxiety, depression, and disconnection, I was able to grow in every area of life. I went from surviving to thriving. From burnout to breakthrough. From a broken marriage to being fully ready for a healthy relationship. From a business of three locations to twenty-five in just a year and a half. None of that came by accident. It came because I chose to do the internal work. And through it all, therapy, especially the wise presence of my therapist, helped light the way.

But therapy wasn't the only invitation into the quiet. My faith, rediscovered in a deeper way at the age of twenty-seven, called me into something just as powerful: stillness. In a world that glorifies hustle and noise, God invited me into silence. Time in the Bible. Time in prayer. Time in reflection. Not stuck or stagnant, but still and searching. That sacred stillness taught me how to examine without shame, how to listen without fear, and how to be with my thoughts without being overtaken by them.

The combination of both faith and therapy became my foundation. They worked together, hand in hand, to help me reconnect with who I really am, not who I am expected to be. It was in the quiet, intentional moments, whether in the therapist's chair or in prayer, that I began to truly hear, not the noise of the world but the whisper of God and the voice of my true self, rising from underneath the weight of everything I had carried. That's where transformation began.

So get comfortable in the silence and comfortable in your own mind. It is there that you will find who you are and where you can begin to learn which of life's pursuits truly will give you purpose, direction, and meaning. Doing that will foster hope and joy when you chase the things that truly matter to you. In my experience, the journey toward obtaining them can be as hopeful and joyful as actually achieving and obtaining them. My life goal example is my family and my freedom. My other example is the opportunity to create Become Unshaken.

Despite what seemed like a lack of time and opportunity, my passion, excitement, and joy in the creation of Become Unshaken allowed me plenty of time to pursue it. I happily made time and found time to pursue what I wanted. And let me testify here and now that the grind of pursuing my dream gave me both hope and joy because I now knew what I wanted and was able to find hope and joy in surviving COVID and divorce. Because I knew what I was striving for, I had hope and joy through the rapid expansion of my restaurants. And because I knew what I was looking for, I was able to take time to be present and focused on developing what would become the single most loving and supportive romantic relationship of my life. None of it was easy. None of the results were

> *For the first time in my life, I knew what I truly wanted. That made enduring the hardships in obtaining them hopeful and filled with joy.*

guaranteed. But because I took the time to escape the world and dive deep into who I was and what I wanted, my goals were clear and purposeful. For the first time in my life, I knew what I truly wanted. That made enduring the hardships in obtaining them hopeful and filled with joy.

For almost three years, I was alone in my house and life half of the time. That facilitated focus and self-analysis, and gave me an opportunity to prepare for the future I wanted. It unified my wants and allowed me to be mentally, emotionally, spiritually, and physically ready for all life had to offer. It led to greater strength and allowed me to create goals that gave me hope and purpose, and a focused plan of attack. Finally, I was understanding what it was that I truly wanted professionally, which was to be a large-scale businessman. It also allowed me to truly know the type of woman I wanted to spend the rest of my life with and pursue those goals with.

I was able to find hope and joy during a global crisis where loneliness, despair, and fear were commonplace. I was able to take an unprecedented global crisis and permanently alter my future and the future of my family. This time of solitude, stillness, and reflection was when I was finally able to recognize, create, and live the values I hope to teach and instill in you. It is not easy, but nothing of value ever is. That is why my mission is to help others find hope and joy in the difficult times of life. Hope and joy allow you to remain unflinching and immovable.

If you've never practiced silence intentionally, it may feel uncomfortable at first. You might get antsy. You might even feel like you're wasting time. You're not. You're planting seeds that will eventually bear incredible fruit.

My Experience with Silence

When I first started practicing silence, it wasn't a pretty scene. My mind raced. I thought about deadlines, dinner plans, bills, you name it. At times, it felt pointless. But slowly, as I stayed faithful to the process, things began to change. In the stillness, I began to hear the real cries of my heart—dreams I had buried under years of survival-mode living. I discovered that I had a deep desire to lead others to hope. That I wanted to create, not just consume. That I was called to build, not just exist. And perhaps most importantly, I realized that many of the things I thought I wanted were really just echoes of other people's expectations, not the genuine desires of my own soul. Silence gave me clarity. It gave me direction. It gave me the foundation I needed to start building a life of real purpose, anchored in joy.

Before we dive into the values that have helped me endure and thrive, I want you to take a bold step. Commit to finding comfort in silence. The strategies I'll share with you are powerful, yes, but they are tools, not destinations. You have to know what you are building toward. You have to know the dreams and desires that have been uniquely placed in your heart. Otherwise, you may end up climbing a ladder, only to realize it's leaning against the wrong wall. I want more for you than that. I want you to live with joy, purpose, and hope, even when life gets hard. And it all begins in the quiet.

Practical Steps

1. *Chill on the Media*

   Too often we find ourselves and our lives bombarded with technology. Whether it is a television always being on, music playing in the car, audiobooks, the incessant scrolling of a phone, or podcasts (yes, even the Become Unshaken Podcast), we are constantly distracting our minds from peace. So, I challenge you to do an audit of your cell phone screen time, television time, and computer and music consumption. Then choose one or two things to cut out for a total of four hours per month. That shouldn't be impossible. The goal is to create time for your own mental recovery. At least once per week I refuse to turn the radio on in my car. Instead, I think and consider. I stop distracting myself and allow my mind to wander. These silent road trips are what helped birth Become Unshaken. Without the stillness, would I have ever found my passion in helping others? Silence bred both healing and purpose for me. Peace of mind led me to my inner desire to help others. The possibilities are endless. Give yourself the chance to discover who you are, have become, and intend to be.

2. *Breathe Often and Appreciate What You Have*
   a. Alternative arts and physical practices such as yoga and Pilates utilize the art of breathing. They calm your body and allow you to focus on your being. Breathe in through the nose and out through the mouth. Find peace and calm through focusing on slowing yourself down. Fill your lungs. Focus.
   b. Now, make a list. Include every blessing you can think of, no matter how big or small. You woke up today. That wasn't guaranteed. Do you care? You should. You were able to get out of bed. You have a place to actually take time in silence. That is a blessing that is not guaranteed for all. Did you have access to education? Can you afford groceries? Is there one friend or family member who knows you, cares for you, and loves you? Appreciate the things you often take for granted. Making a list will snap you back to the reality of your unearned blessings, which is a great way to recenter your heart on what is good. If you appreciate and remember what you have, large and small, you can begin fostering a heart of joy.
3. *Don't Quit*

True transformation doesn't happen overnight. I had to break the habits of twenty years of life. My need for distraction was great. I am a doer. That means when I sat down, I felt guilt. There was always something else to do. Creating this new habit of stillness and acclimation to silence will not be easy. It's simply not the human way. We validate ourselves with the effort we try to show others. My challenge to you is to state your goal to those around you to both hold yourself accountable and also get them on board with your goals. Initially your mind will race. Your tendency to try to grab your phone or "just do one little thing" during that time will shock you. But stay strong. In time you will come to settle. Do not quit.

Chapter 5

PRINCIPLE 2: DEFINE YOUR PURPOSE – PURSUE, PRIORITIZE, PROTECT

If there is one thing I know to be true, it's this: You were made to be passionate about something. Deep down, at your very core, there is a spark of purpose: a fire meant to fuel you through the hard days and inspire you through the good ones. And if you haven't found that yet, keep looking. You must pursue your *why*.

Life is full of obligations. Responsibilities stack up. Whether it's work, bills, parenting, or simply the grind of surviving the week, we often find ourselves buried under the weight of necessity. We take our responsibilities seriously, and we should. But without something to get our hearts racing a bit, to stir our minds, to wake us up with excitement and joy, we risk growing stagnant. So stop reading right here and consider what your purpose is. What, if it were removed from your life, would make it hard to get out of bed?

This isn't just a poetic concern. It's a psychological reality. Studies show that over 280 million people worldwide suffer from depression, and in many cases, it's deeply tied to a sense of purposelessness or a lack of meaningful engagement in life. In the United States alone, nearly one in five adults live with mental illness. That's over 59 million people, and research consistently links the absence of purpose to increased levels of anxiety, hopelessness, and depressive symptoms. Without a clear sense of *why*, we risk waking up one day and realizing we've lost our sense of wonder. That's not how we were made to live.

And if that's not enough to support the importance of purpose, let me take it one step further. In his book *Mission Possible: Go Create a Life That Counts*, Tim Tebow references a meta-analysis published in *Psychosomatic Medicine: Journal of Biobehavioral Medicine* that examined the purpose in life and mortality. The study found that "people without a strong life purpose were more than twice as likely to die between the study years of 2006 and 2010, compared with those who had one."

The meta-analysis, called "Purpose in Life and Its Relationship to All-Cause Mortality and Cardiovascular Events: A Meta-Analysis," pooled data from over 136,000 adults (with an average age of sixty-seven) across ten studies in the United States and Japan. Those with a high sense of purpose had about a 20 percent lower risk of all-cause mortality and reduced cardiovascular events.

Life reminds us that there's meaning in more than just pushing through. We're meant to find joy in the effort itself. We weren't made just to survive but to feel alive in the work and the moments that make up our days. The gift is in the living, not just the striving. So if your work feels stale, if your spirit feels dry, maybe it's time to dig deeper. To explore. To pursue something that awakens you.

For me, writing started as a whisper, a small idea to capture some of my story for my children. It was a private project, a quiet pursuit meant for the people I love most. But as I began to write, a new energy emerged. The more I poured onto the page, the more alive I felt. This was more than a chore. This was joy. This was something I looked forward to. And soon, what was for them began to bless me, and now I want to bless you too.

The beauty of passion is that it breathes new life into everything else. It's not about abandoning responsibilities; it's about elevating them. When you find something that excites you, it makes you a better parent, spouse, friend, and professional. It replenishes what stress and fatigue try to steal. It anchors you again in joy, the Unshaken kind, rooted not in fleeting happiness but in a deep, soul-level engagement for what is possible.

So I ask you: What is your purpose? What lights you up? What do you do that makes the time disappear? If you haven't found it yet, don't dare settle. Keep looking. Try something new. Volunteer. Paint. Mentor someone. Coach. Build something. Start a garden. Write a story. Learn an instrument. Go back to school. Go forward in faith. Perhaps you should consider a career change. Changing from a job that feels unfulfilling to one aligned with personal passions and values can have significant benefits for mental health.

Research shows that individuals who feel a sense of purpose and intrinsic motivation in their work experience lower levels of stress, anxiety, and depression. In fact, a study published in the

Journal of Occupational and Environmental Medicine found that employees engaged in meaningful work reported higher levels of psychological well-being and life satisfaction. Additionally, people who shift into careers that better reflect their identity and passions often experience increased energy, improved self-esteem, and stronger resilience to workplace challenges. While career transitions can be daunting, the mental health gains of doing work that matters to you often outweigh the short-term discomfort of change.

Whatever it is, it doesn't have to be big. It just has to be yours.

Your passions aren't distractions from your purpose. They're often the clearest signs of it. If your daily routine feels more like a burden than a calling, it might be time to pause and reconnect with what energizes you. Stay open to what stirs your curiosity or lights you up. And when that passion reveals itself, lean in. Let it become a source of daily renewal. A reminder that joy is possible, even in the midst of chaos.

An Unshaken life isn't one without storms. It's one with roots deep enough to outlast them. And passion? Passion is part of what keeps those roots strong.

> *An Unshaken life isn't one without storms. It's one with roots deep enough to outlast them.*

So find your *why*. Fuel it with something that sets your soul on fire. And never stop pursuing a life that brings you hope, fills you with joy, and leads you back again and again to the unshakable truth that you were made for more.

Before I dive into my *why*, I want to address a common *why* that so many have, especially our younger generation who are absent the responsibilities of a family and children. I have learned that all things can be good. We are not expected to live as martyrs, purposefully restricting ourselves from all things material. A beautiful painting, an outfit, a handbag, or a brand-new pair of Jordans have merit as good. The perfectly cooked meal, a beautiful and powerful vehicle, and a home are all worthy pursuits and opportunities to celebrate life's goodness. But beware of seeking material possessions as the *why* you pursue and take joy in.

When material possessions become the foundation of our *why*, we anchor ourselves to something inherently unstable and fleeting. It's easy to believe that a new car, a bigger house, or the latest technology will bring lasting happiness. The joy they bring is temporary and often superficial. The danger lies in building a life around things that can be lost, stolen, or outgrown. Things that ultimately have no enduring impact on our deepest sense of joy, purpose, or identity. Jim Carrey once said, "I think everybody should get rich and famous and do everything they ever dreamed of so they can see that it's not the answer." Despite achieving every worldly success, Carrey was left feeling empty, revealing the illusion that possessions can satisfy the soul.

Many others have echoed this truth. No matter how much we accumulate, the soul longs for something more substantial—meaning, connection, and purpose. When we chase things that can never truly fill us, we are left exhausted and disoriented, searching for lasting fulfillment in temporary places.

To live an Unshaken life means choosing a deeper *why*. One rooted in purpose, character, connection, and faith. These are things that can't be taken from you and don't fade with time. Anchoring your life to what truly matters provides stability when circumstances shift and when possessions inevitably lose their shine. When your foundation is built on values that transcend material wealth, you find a sense of joy and peace that things alone could never provide. Choose better. Choose meaning. Choose to be unwavering with regard to pursuing and then prioritizing your why, for your why is your purpose. It is the North Star of your life's journey.

> *Choose to be unwavering with regard to pursuing and then prioritizing your why, for your why is your purpose. It is the North Star of your life's journey.*

The *Why* of Work

Family is my *why*. They are the reason I wake up, strive, and sacrifice. That's true for many people We will discuss this more, but first, let's dive into those whose deepest sense of purpose is not rooted in family but in vocation. What if your career is the space where your soul lights up, where you feel most connected to your calling? That, too, is a valid and honorable pursuit. When your work aligns with your values and contributes to the betterment of others, it becomes more than a paycheck. It becomes your mission field.

Yet it's important to recognize that not all work automatically qualifies as a lasting or meaningful purpose. A career pursued solely for status, money, or momentary satisfaction can become a fragile foundation. Jobs can be lost. Titles can fade. Industries can collapse. That's why a true *why* must be anchored in soul-deep purpose, something that continues even when circumstances change. It's work that supports the well-being of others, uplifts communities, restores broken systems, and reflects values that endure beyond personal gain.

Research confirms the importance of purpose in work. According to a 2022 study by McKinsey & Company, 70 percent of employees said their sense of purpose is defined by their work, and those who feel connected to the mission of their organization are five times more likely to remain engaged and fulfilled. Moreover, a Deloitte study found that 73 percent of employees who say they work for a purpose-driven organization are satisfied with their jobs, compared to just 23 percent in organizations without a strong mission. When work reflects shared values, employees don't just perform better; they live with more hope, resilience, and joy.

Take, for example, someone who works for Habitat for Humanity. Their day-to-day tasks, whether swinging a hammer, managing logistics, or writing grants, serve a greater purpose: providing homes for families in need. Each action has a tangible, soul-level impact. Their job isn't just work; it's a form of justice, compassion, and restoration. That kind of purpose is sustainable even through hard days because it is bigger than the individual. It connects directly to the human spirit's longing for significance.

Or consider a hypothetical example: a graphic designer who partners with nonprofits to create campaigns for mental health awareness. Their *why* isn't just about design excellence; it's about storytelling that heals. Their talents are tools for spreading hope, breaking stigmas, and changing lives. Even if projects change or clients shift, the deeper mission remains intact. That's what makes it a valid and lasting *why*. It's not temporary happiness but enduring impact.

That doesn't mean everyone has to work for a nonprofit or humanitarian cause. Your career could be in tech, education, business, healthcare, or the arts. The key is alignment. When your personal values and passions match the values and mission of your work. A schoolteacher pouring into the lives of children, a nurse advocating for underserved patients, an entrepreneur building ethical, sustainable businesses. Each of these professionals has a career *why* that contributes to something far bigger than themselves.

So when you consider your purpose, don't overlook your work. But don't stop at surface-level motivation either. Ask yourself, "Does my work reflect something of eternal value? Does it bring light to others, promote justice, foster healing, or advance human dignity?" If so, then your career is not only a valid purpose; it is a sacred one. And in that sacred pursuit, you will find hope and joy that remain Unshaken, even when the world around you shifts.

Family First – The *Why* That Grounds Me

If there was one truth I knew deep down long before I had a degree, a job, or a five-year plan, it was this: I wanted to be a father. Not just any father but a present one, a loving one, a father worthy of admiration and trust. While other kids were dreaming of being astronauts, I was dreaming of playing superheroes in the living room and carrying sleeping kids to bed. My younger brother, Joseph, might argue that I stepped into the role a bit early. I had taken to "parenting" him before I was even old enough to stay home alone. What can I say? It was written into the deepest part of me. Family would be my purpose.

The year was 2002, and I was just beginning my freshman year at the University of Illinois Urbana-Champaign. At that time, the college had the largest Greek population of fraternities and sororities in the United States. That being the case, I decided to do something I never would have imagined and decided to rush. Upon being offered an opportunity to pledge at *Phi Sigma Kappa*, I began the process of trying to join. One plug I will make is that this fraternity was non-hazing, which is the only way I would have joined. I made it clear up front that nobody who wanted to call themselves my brother would have me do things that went against my character or beliefs. I told them that mistreating me because I wanted to join and then treating me differently and better as a result wasn't going to fly. Thankfully, none of that happened. However, there was a night that I will never forget, and for all the right and comical reasons.

The fraternity had an evening where all the pledges, I believe there were around eighteen of us, were called to meet on the main floor and face the brothers. We were lined up facing the crowd of almost sixty, unsure of what was about to happen. I believe I was around the fifteenth pledge in line. One by one, they asked, "What do you want more than anything right now?" And one by one, we got it wrong. I will let each of you reading this imagine what a bunch of eighteen-year-old boys would answer if they were given a magic genie to grant them just one wish. But for this group of sixty or so college-aged, prospective fraternal brothers, all answers were wrong. Then it was my turn.

I was absolutely positive that I had the right answer. I was sure that they wanted a heartfelt, soul-filling, truthful answer. It was an answer that was going to blow them away and solve the riddle, and we'd be released from what began to feel like an interrogation. They had just screamed "No!" to the fourteenth answer, and now it was my turn. They asked me, "What do you want more than anything right now?" I screamed at the top of my lungs, "A wife and kids!" You have never heard a frat house quieter in your life. What did this kid with the giant chain and fake diamond earrings just yell (yeah, I was super cool)? Who was this kid who impersonated Usher at every party? You could hear a pin drop. And just like a movie, after what felt like an hour and was probably closer to five seconds, a quiet voice in the back corner of the room said, "No?" Sixty college kids were flabbergasted. Never has there been a more "uncollege" thing said in the history of college. So, like I said, becoming a family man was my deep soul desire from a very young age.

In 2011, that dream began to take form when I became a father for the first time, albeit unexpectedly. A casual relationship led to an unplanned pregnancy. I was beginning my dream of fatherhood in a way I had never imagined, with a woman I hardly knew. What ensued was a heartbreaking battle over custody and parental roles. Navigating new parenthood is a struggle for everyone, but to do it with a person you know very little about led to a lack of trust, a lot of misunderstanding, and significant difficulty.

The first six months of my son's life were some of the most painful I've ever endured. During that entire time, I saw him less than twenty-four hours, not because I didn't want to be there but because I couldn't. I was caught in the slow, grinding gears of a legal system that seemed more interested in procedures than people. I waited on local courts and due process, trapped in a kind of limbo where each day without him felt like an eternity. It wasn't just the waiting; it was not knowing.

Before I could even hold the title "father" in the eyes of the law, I was required to first prove paternity. Though there was no doubt he was mine, the law demanded paperwork, testing, and time. Time I would never get back. That process, compounded by decisions made by all those involved, along with the inevitable delays of legal bureaucracy, kept me at arm's length from my own child.

It's important to say this: His mother was navigating her own fears and challenges, and while many of her actions hurt me deeply, I don't write this to villainize her. I believe most people do the best they can with what they know in moments of crisis, and I know now that she was struggling too. But still, there is no easy way to reconcile a heart that longs to hold their child but is told to wait.

Finally, when paternity was legally recognized, I was granted the chance to be with my son—half the time. Half. And while some might see that as a compromise, to me it was a miracle. From the moment I held my son in my arms for the first time, something eternal shifted in me. It wasn't just emotional; it was spiritual. Life no longer revolved around my ambitions or my pain. In that sacred moment, I discovered my *why*. It wasn't a goal to achieve but a calling to answer. Fatherhood became my center, and from that day forward, nothing has ever been the same.

We will talk a lot in this book about knowing your *why*, that deeply rooted purpose that helps you remain Unshaken through life's storms. For me, after the birth of my first son, my *why* would begin and end with my family. My wife and children are not just priorities; they are the reason the rest of my priorities exist. They are the core of every business move, every early morning grind, every late-night decision. But here's the key: Providing financially is the lowest form of provision. Presence is more powerful than any other. My business doesn't just exist to make money; it exists to create freedom. Freedom to show up for games, be home for dinner, pray with my kids at night, and laugh on Saturday mornings over French toast.

Let me speak directly for a moment to all those business owners out there. Entrepreneurship can be a beautiful path and opportunity to steward talents and resources well. But it can also be a trap. The world will tell you to hustle harder, work later, and always be "on." But if we're not careful, we'll end up building something impressive on the outside while our families are starving for our presence on the inside. I've seen too many people achieve worldly success and still feel empty. Why? Because they lost sight of who they were doing it for.

I decided early that my business would not cost me my family. It would not rob my children of a father. It would not distract me from the ministry I'm most called to, the one that begins within the four walls of my home. I won't always get it right, but I can make intentional choices like muting my phone on Sundays. Like playing superheroes with my son. Like shooting buckets with my big boys. Like leaving my office to attend my girl's impromptu gymnastic performances. Like taking my wife on dates or throwing a Barbie Dream House dance party right before bedtime. Like teaching my children that they matter more than the business. If I died today, I know I will have done all I could to make sure all my family knew they were not only my *why* but were also prioritized and protected.

Passion vs. Purpose

Stephanie's professional track record is remarkable by any standard. Over her twenty-year career in the pharmaceutical and healthcare space, she has led in learning and development, sales, and human resources, and she has even served as a strategic advisor. She's been responsible for critical people strategies and transformational initiatives because of her rare ability to combine strategy, innovation, and passion for people development. What she builds doesn't just work; it changes how people feel about work. Her professional life reflects a deep, contagious passion for developing others, shaping culture, and breathing new life into the environments she's part of. And she loves it, not just the outcomes but the creative process, the problem-solving, and the progress. Her career has been both a laboratory for her gifts and a runway for her passions.

But here's what sets Stephanie apart. She doesn't confuse her passion with her purpose. She knows the difference because she has spent time in silence to wrestle with it. Silence reveals what the noise of ambition can't. In stillness, she's come to understand that her career, as fulfilling as it is, is not the center of her life. Family is. Purpose, for Stephanie, is found in the laughter of her children, her dedication to our marriage, the unseen sacrifices made at home, and the sacred work of showing up fully not just at the office, but around the dinner table. That truth anchors her in a world where positions are temporary and titles are rented. What matters most can't be promoted or posted. It has to be lived.

Stephanie isn't motivated by recognition, although she's earned it. She's driven by what her work makes possible:

stability for her family, flexibility to show up where it matters, and the ability to pour back into the people she loves. That distinction between passion and purpose is what allows her to rise even when the weight of the world tries to keep her down. She doesn't have to sacrifice joy for success. Her passion sparks momentum, but purpose sustains it. And Stephanie knows exactly what hers is. In the quiet, she found clarity. And with that clarity, she lives in a way that's both high-achieving and deeply grounded, living out her passion while remaining grounded in her purpose.

Presence over Perfection

Being a parent is hard. Being a spouse is hard. You'll mess up. You'll say the wrong thing, miss the mark, and get too busy. But being present doesn't mean being perfect. It means showing up. It means making it a priority again and again. It means hugging your family even when they've messed up. It means listening when you're tired. It means choosing their recital over your inbox. And it means knowing that the legacy you're leaving isn't about the secondary things you built, accomplished, or pursued but about the love and time you prioritized.

When I think about what it means to live Unshaken, it's not just about enduring hardship; it's about planting yourself so deeply in your purpose that you cannot be moved. For me, that purpose is my family. They are my anchor, my joy, and my reason. And every decision I make in business, in life, and in faith is filtered through that truth.

So here's my challenge to you: If you haven't already done this, define and then pursue your *why*. Write it down. Speak it out loud. Revisit it regularly. And if your *why* includes your family, then let your calendar reflect that. Let your energy reflect that. Let your joy flow out of those precious relationships. Make it your priority.

There will always be more work, more opportunities, and more deadlines. But you only get one life to raise your kids, build a marriage worth having, and show the people you love what truly matters. This is where protecting it comes in. The last thing any of us want is missed time and moments we can't get back.

Still, let's be honest. It's not as if you only get one shot to do it perfectly. That's not quite true. You'll mess up. You'll lose your temper, miss the mark, and get distracted. But the beauty of this life is that it gives us countless chances to turn back, try again, and recommit to what matters most. You don't have to live perfectly; you just have to live intentionally.

So choose presence, even when you've been absent. Choose love, even when it's hard. Choose joy, even when the weight is heavy.

And when you fall—because we all do—get back up and choose again.

> *So choose presence, even when you've been absent. Choose love, even when it's hard. Choose joy, even when the weight is heavy.*

Practical Steps

1. *Reflect on What Energizes You*
   Think back to the moments when you felt most alive. When time seemed to fly and you walked away feeling more filled up than drained. What were you doing?

Who were you with? Often, the things that energize us are windows into what we're made for. These aren't just hobbies or good memories; they're clues. When you trace those moments over time, patterns begin to emerge that can point you toward your core passions and values. Pay close attention. Your *why* might already be in motion, waiting to be noticed.

2. *Make Space to Explore*

   Purpose doesn't usually reveal itself in the chaos of back-to-back meetings or in the marginless hustle of daily demands. If your life is jammed wall-to-wall, it's nearly impossible to hear your heart speak. That's why finding your *why* requires margin—space to breathe, reflect, and try. You don't need to quit your job or take a sabbatical. Just start with a few hours a week to explore something new or revisit a past interest. Think of it like clearing a field before planting. The seed of purpose needs room to grow. Without space, even the most meaningful ideas can suffocate under the weight of "busy."

3. *Listen to the Whispers*

   Purpose rarely arrives with fanfare. More often, it shows up in quiet nudges, those recurring ideas, gut feelings, or daydreams that refuse to go away. They're easy to dismiss because they seem small or impractical, but those whispers often carry the voice of calling. Start paying attention to what stirs in you when the noise dies down. What keeps tugging at your heart? Instead of pushing it aside, sit with it. Ask what it might be trying to show you.

4. *Engage in Joyful Experimentation*

   You don't need to have it all figured out before you take the first step. Sometimes your *why* is uncovered through trying, failing, laughing, and learning. Write, build, paint, coach, volunteer. Whatever sparks your curiosity or stirs delight. Don't worry about being good at it; instead, focus on how it makes you feel while you're doing it. Joyful experimentation is how many people stumble into their purpose, by simply doing things that make their soul come alive. Let curiosity lead the way.

5. *Ask the Right Questions*

   Clarity often comes not from answers but from the right questions. What do you do that makes time disappear? What fills you up so deeply that you'd pursue it even if no one ever noticed or applauded? What would you regret not trying? These questions dig beneath surface desires and begin to reveal the values and passions that shape your true *why*. Ask them often, and answer with honesty. You may be surprised by what rises to the top.

6. *Pay Attention to What Replenishes You*

   The things that restore you aren't just self-care; they're signals. Pay attention to what makes you a better friend, parent, or professional. Notice what leaves you refreshed, more patient, more generous, more you. When you're aligned with your *why*, your life doesn't feel like one long drain; instead, it starts to flow. Passion and purpose don't exhaust you; they replenish you. Lean into the things that fuel your joy and resilience. That's usually a good sign you're getting closer to the life you were meant to live.

Chapter 6

BUILD YOUR LIFE ON UNSHAKEN VALUES

O ver the last thirty years through every hardship, failure, success, and season of waiting, four values have consistently risen to the surface of my life throughout my current journey. They weren't given to me all at once. I learned them through trial and error, through mistakes and moments of mercy, and through valleys and victories.

Those principles are not magic formulas. They won't eliminate pain. They won't guarantee perfect outcomes. But they will give you a foundation that is strong enough to withstand the toughest seasons of your life. They will point you toward joy when everything around you seems to demand despair. And they will equip you to live not just as a survivor but as someone who thrives.

To live a life that endures the storms and celebrates true success, we must be firmly anchored to values that do not shift with circumstances. These values are more than good intentions. They are the habits of heart and mind that shape who we become. When challenges arise, it's not fleeting feelings or short-lived motivation that keep us grounded. It's the deeper commitments we've made to our core values and sense of purpose. Anchoring yourself in what truly matters isn't just defense against the trials of life; it's the foundation for a life filled with meaning, joy, and lasting impact.

> *Anchoring yourself in what truly matters isn't just defense against the trials of life; it's the foundation for a life filled with meaning, joy, and lasting impact.*

At the heart of these values is an unrelenting work ethic—working hard not merely for recognition or reward but because effort itself shapes and prepares us. Every hour we spend in diligent work, even when no one notices, sharpens our skills and deepens our character. There is blessing in the work, whether or not the results are immediate. Hard work sows seeds for future opportunities, aligning us with the truth that we are being prepared for blessings we cannot yet see. In this way, the process itself becomes sacred. A quiet offering that draws us closer to our best selves.

Equally vital is the commitment to live with restraint and discipline. In a culture that encourages instant gratification and constant consumption, choosing self-control is a radical act of strength. Financially, emotionally, and physically we are called to deny short-term pleasures when they do not serve our long-term good. Resisting the pull of fleeting desires allows us to experience a deeper, more satisfying joy, the kind of joy that grows slowly but surely as we build for the future. Discipline is not about deprivation; it is about honoring the bigger vision we hold, trusting that the beauty of lasting achievement far outweighs any temporary thrill.

It's about aligning our daily choices with the future we truly want, not just what feels good in the moment.

When faced with a decision, it's easy to default to what brings instant gratification. But a powerful way to center yourself is to pause and ask, "Will I be proud of this choice tomorrow? In a month? A year?" True discipline invites us to look beyond fleeting impulses and consider the long-term consequences of our actions. It challenges us to build a life that isn't just enjoyable now but deeply fulfilling over time. Choosing discipline isn't about saying no to pleasure. It's about saying yes to a life of purpose, integrity, and enduring satisfaction.

Patience, too, is an essential anchor, especially in the struggles of life. There are seasons when progress feels slow, prayers seem unanswered, and hope feels stretched thin. Yet it is in those moments that patience becomes a quiet declaration of faith, a trust that God's timing is perfect, even when we cannot see the full picture. Waiting well is not passive; it is an active choice to lean into trust, allowing our souls to be shaped and strengthened as we hold fast to the belief that every delay has purpose.

Finally, the resolve to get up and push forward, no matter the obstacle, is a value that breathes life into all the others. Life will knock us down. Disappointments and hardships are inevitable. But what defines us is not the fall. It is the choice to rise again and do so with joy and hope in our hearts. That kind of resilience reflects a deep faith that we are never walking alone and that every new day holds the promise of grace and growth. When we anchor ourselves in these values, we become people who are not only Unshaken by life's storms but also radiant with joy and strength that can inspire others.

Each of these values is rooted deeply in both practical experience and biblical truth. Each one has a story attached—a real, raw moment in my life where the principle was tested and either proved true or had to be painfully learned. My goal is to be as vulnerable and honest with you as possible.

If we are going to walk this road together, you deserve the truth—the good, the bad, and the hard-earned wisdom from it all. Adopting the Unshaken Values—work ethic, patience, discipline, and perseverance—runs against the grain of a culture obsessed with

> *Adopting the Unshaken Values—work ethic, patience, discipline, and perseverance—runs against the grain of a culture obsessed with shortcuts, instant gratification, and surface-level success.*

shortcuts, instant gratification, and surface-level success. Living with an Unshaken Mindset is not always easy. These values ask more of you. They require depth in a world of distractions and endurance in a society addicted to ease. Without first grounding yourself in silence and understanding your true purpose, these values will feel like a burden rather than a breakthrough. Silence is where clarity is born. It's where you meet the unfiltered version of yourself and confront the *why* behind your actions. When you begin from that place of purpose, the Unshaken Values no longer feel like impossible ideals. They become natural extensions of who you are.

This path won't always be smooth. You'll wrestle with old habits, face doubts, and question if it's worth it. That's all part of the process. Give yourself grace because growth is gritty. But take heart. With each act of disciplined effort, each patient step, and each moment you choose perseverance over comfort, hope begins to rise. Joy takes root, not from ease but from the strength you uncover along the way. The Unshaken life isn't about perfection; it's about becoming. And every time you return to your purpose in silence, those values will grow stronger within you.

Remaining steadfast in these values is not a lofty ideal. It's the key skill for living with joy and finding success. When we decide to hold fast to our values, no matter the circumstances, it's easy to become discouraged early on by the challenges we face along the way. The journey often feels long, and the work can be grueling. However, we must recognize that there is immense strength in maintaining our values, especially when life pushes us to the edge. In fact, over time, the very challenges that test our resolve are what ultimately refine us, shape our character, and lead us to the success we've been working toward.

Remaining steadfast isn't about avoiding the tough times; it's about choosing joy and purpose, even when the going gets tough. Think about farmers. Their work is often done in the dirt, unseen and underappreciated, but the seeds they plant, nurture, and care for grow into something beautiful. Something that will provide nourishment, shelter, and beauty for years to come. Similarly, when we stay true to our values, we are planting seeds of integrity, work ethic, and resilience that will bloom into the fruits of our labor. We can find familial joy or professional satisfaction. It's easy to get distracted by short-term rewards, but true joy comes from long-term, consistent effort and a deep-rooted commitment to our values.

It's not always glamorous to remain steadfast. Often, we must make choices that may seem inconvenient or even difficult in the moment, but they shape who we are and what we become. Over time, our persistence becomes our greatest asset, and with it comes the joy of knowing that we've stayed true to what matters most.

But there's an important warning here. Persistence and wisdom must walk hand in hand. Not every battle is worth fighting, and not every path is worth staying on. There's a fine line between perseverance and plain stubbornness—a refusal to pivot, adapt, or learn from failure. Where persistence is rooted in clarity and conviction, stubbornness is often rooted in pride or fear. If we're not careful, we can wear ourselves out chasing something that no longer serves our purpose, mistaking rigidity for faithfulness. So how do we tell the difference?

Start by examining the impact of your persistence. Is it leading to growth, peace, or meaningful progress? Or is it draining you, isolating you, and leading to repeated frustration with little return? Second, invite trusted voices into the conversation. I'll discuss this more later, but your tribe—your most trusted confidants—can be one of your greatest and most useful assets. Wise counsel often sees blind spots we cannot. Third, ask yourself if the resistance you're facing is external (temporary challenges) or internal (a nagging sense that something is off). Lastly, remain open to the possibility that letting go is not failure. It may actually be the most courageous, faithful next step you can take.

Being Unshaken doesn't mean being immovable in every situation. It means staying rooted in what matters most while staying humble and wise enough to change course when needed.

In the face of difficulty, it's tempting to compromise our values for a quick win or an easier path. It is when the business owner looks for a way to cut costs but reduces the quality they expect of their product. A life that is Unshaken doesn't lean on shortcuts. It stands on character, even when it's costly. A coworker who takes credit for work they did not do betrays the trust of the team in an effort to get ahead. An Unshaken life means holding to your principles even when that means harder work and a longer road, not to mention that the joy we experience from those shortcuts is fleeting. More likely is the possibility that it creates a more natural response to do those things again. It normalizes the easy road built and forged on the opposite of your values. It builds a house of cards that can fall during that first quality inspection or conversation with your boss.

On the other hand, when we choose to stick with our principles and values, whether in business, relationships, or personal growth, the joy we feel when we reach the other side is profound. It's the kind of joy that comes from knowing we've done things the right way, regardless of the external circumstances or results.

It's easy to recognize this truth in the lives of those who have achieved remarkable success. Their paths weren't smooth or free from obstacles, but what sets them apart is their unwavering ability to remain committed through the challenges. Take an elite athlete, for example. Their training is grueling, often repetitive, and filled with moments where motivation is nowhere to be found. But they press on, not because it's easy but because they understand that discipline, not emotion, drives results.

Consider the Mamba Mentality of Kobe Bryant. He once said, "Those times when you get up early, and you work hard, those times when you stay up late, and you work hard, those times when you don't feel like working, you're too tired, you don't want to push yourself, but you do it anyway. That is actually the dream. That's the dream. It's not the destination; it's the journey. And if you guys can understand that, then what you'll see happen is you won't accomplish your dreams; your dreams won't come true; something greater will." Kobe's mindset wasn't built on chasing greatness; it was forged through relentless commitment to the fundamentals. He outworked everyone else, not just in the spotlight but in the unseen hours. It is in the mundane, exhausting, overlooked moments where most give up. That's what made him a legend.

Or take it from arguably the greatest Olympian of all time, Michael Phelps. He once said, "I think with practice, you can become whatever you want to be, and with a goal you can go in any direction that you want to go in." Phelps was so disciplined that he trained every day for years. No breaks, not even on Christmas. His coach, Bob Bowman, emphasized that Phelps' strength wasn't just in his physical ability but in his commitment to doing the same work day after day with unwavering focus. That consistency became his greatest weapon.

So success is not only about grit; it's also about momentum. When you're just beginning, it can feel like you're pushing a boulder uphill. But once movement starts, even small steps create a force of their own. Momentum turns effort into progress and progress into motivation. Psychologist Jordan Peterson teaches that negotiating with yourself compassionately is key to sustaining that momentum. Rather than driving yourself with self-criticism and harsh expectations, Peterson's Rule 2 says, "Treat yourself like someone you are responsible for helping." If you're always cracking the whip, your mind will start to resist— even procrastinate—as a form of self-protection. But if you build trust with yourself through achievable goals and self-respect, you'll generate enough positive energy to spiral upward rather than fall behind. That kind of momentum doesn't just carry you forward. It lifts you, renews you, and keeps you steadfast when everything else tells you to quit.

The same principle applies to all areas of life. The work may be hard, but the rewards are worth it.

Building Resilience: The Joy Found in Perseverance

Perseverance isn't just about pushing through challenges; it's about learning and growing through adversity. When we choose to stand firm in our values, we develop a resilience that becomes a source of strength, not only for ourselves but for others as well. As we overcome obstacles, we build a foundation of wisdom and experience that allows us to handle even greater challenges with grace and confidence.

Moreover, our resilience becomes an example to others. When others see us remain steadfast in our values, even when it's difficult, we inspire them to do the same. This is how joy spreads: Through our actions, others are encouraged to hold fast to their own values, knowing that they, too, can achieve greatness through hard work and persistence. We don't just find joy in our personal success; we find joy in the impact we have on others as they see our commitment and are motivated to stay true to their own principles. Staying grounded in strong values such as work ethic, honesty, and perseverance brings lasting fulfillment, not fleeting praise.

This lesson translates to every area of life. Success doesn't always go to the most talented. It goes to those who work the hardest and stay steadfast. Discipline breeds results.

Chapter 7

VALUE 1: GRIND BEFORE GLORY

I understand that this is a controversial way to start a discussion on the values I have held dear in my pursuit of joy and success, but I also believe it is foundational for the way I attack each and every pursuit. In life, there are no participation trophies. Either a person achieves their goals or they fail. An objective at work or at home is reached and completed, or it is not. If we show up to work today an hour late, forget to attend a meeting, leave work early, and then skip on making dinner for the family, is anyone going to tell us, "Hey, thanks for showing up?" Unless there is an alternative universe I'm unaware of, the answer is a resounding no. Simply showing up does not get rewarded as an adult.

Then why would we reward this behavior anywhere else? Our goal as people, employees, family members, and parents is to be prepared for the demands of life, and to help raise and lead others around us to be competent and capable in the same way. Anyone can show up. But to be different, you must have the necessary work ethic to earn results, rewards, a raise, prestige, and acknowledgement for a job well done. You don't believe me? Take the words of John Wooden, arguably the best college basketball coach of all time. "Failing to prepare is preparing to fail." If you don't work, don't grind, and don't prepare, you can't expect to achieve positive results or goals. If you're struggling to find joy in what you're doing, it doesn't always mean you're in the wrong place, but it may be time to take a closer look. Sometimes the breakthrough we're longing for isn't about changing direction but about changing how deeply we're committed to the path we're already on. Many people chase results without ever truly giving their best. They rush the process, cut corners, or simply show up without heart. Of course, this isn't everyone. Some give their all and still find themselves waiting on outcomes they have set out to achieve. But for most, joy and success aren't absent because they're unreachable. They're just waiting on the other side of honest, sustained effort. You see, accomplishment after preparation and hard work actually brings joy. Something that comes easily or is given only satisfies momentarily. If I beat my five-year-old in a game of chess, I get very little joy from that. However, if I take months to craft the blueprint for my company of 200 employees and see it come to fruition and generate success, I have immense joy. It's a joy I can feel every time I see it executed. Hard work may seem less than fun in the moment, but recognizing the fruits of your labor can generate lasting joy.

For three summers when I came home from college, I had what I believe was the greatest summer job imaginable. I was a lifeguard for apartment complexes. Believe me, there were hours upon hours that the pools were empty, so my job was getting paid for reading books, listening to music, and working on my tan. It was phenomenal, and I encourage all young adults to do it. However, as a lifeguard, every summer I had ten to twelve saves, which meant that for one reason or another, I was forced to get in the pool to save a child from potentially drowning.

They included kids under the age of two who were floating in a ring, inadvertently flipped over, and got stuck upside down with no ability to get upright. No parent was around to see it. The scariest of these was during an incredibly busy day that led to a young boy forgetting he couldn't swim and jumping in after his friends, immediately sinking to the bottom and chugging the pool water the entire way down. The poor boy sank like a rock and consumed so much water in such a short period of time that I had to push on his stomach to get him to puke the water out. Those kinds of crises happened more often than I would have ever imagined. I had the highest save total in the entire company. One time my boss joked and asked if I was throwing kids in. I promise you, I was not.

The point here is that even in a job that many take lightly, a job that offers a tan and a check, I diligently searched and oversaw the pool. I focused on the purpose of my presence. I was there to make sure nobody got hurt, nobody went unaccounted for, and all rules were followed. When there was a potential save scenario, I recognized it immediately and responded without hesitation. It was a character trait I would hold onto throughout my professional career, regardless of the job or position. Simply put, I was not necessarily better at my job than anyone else, but I worked harder, remained focused, and earned my paycheck.

We all know someone who works in the opposite manner. They are the person you never want to get teamed up with on a class project or plan a work presentation with. They are the last person on earth you want to serve you food at a restaurant. But my contention is that a disciplined, steadfast, focused, work ethic breeds elevated results in any industry or realm of life. Success is never guaranteed, but a strong work ethic drastically improves the likelihood of desired results. That is true for a workout plan, a diet, a business, a startup, parenting, or coaching.

Things given do not feed the soul. False accolades are patronizing. When we are handed praise we didn't earn, something deep inside us knows the difference. The soul senses the void where real effort and growth should be. There simply is not a better feeling than working hard and achieving a goal. An earned win, even if imperfect, builds confidence and character that no handout ever could. Consider the kiddo who gets whatever they want simply by asking. Are they happy? Are they content or appreciative? No. They simply get what they want only to look around for the next thing they can be upset about not having until someone gives it to them again.

Over time, the reward loses its meaning. A "B" earned through struggle holds far more value than an "A" handed over without merit. We don't grow when things come easily. We grow when we persevere, fail, and rise. True satisfaction comes not from ease but from overcoming. When we chase perfection, we often miss purpose. But when we strive, fall short, and still move forward, real progress happens. Appreciation is devoid in entitlement, but it is abundant in earned success. So make lofty goals and set out to achieve them, not for the applause but for the internal strength and joy that come from knowing that you did the work and it mattered.

Terry Crews—actor, television host, and former professional football player—once mentioned a mentality that illustrates the mindset behind work ethic. After retiring from professional football, he was left in a state of uncertainty. He found himself working odd jobs for quite some time as he sought after his next professional chapter. Crews found himself as a janitor and a security guard, and while those jobs probably sound like a downgrade, he transformed himself. His mentality in that part of his life is probably what led to his current success.

Crews decided to work every job, regardless of title or position, as if he was getting paid a million dollars to do it. What would that look like for you? What would working as a janitor and getting paid a million dollars be like? What would you be willing to do to secure and succeed at your job? Perhaps you're an Uber driver, a teacher, a karate instructor, or a construction worker. If your boss was paying you a million dollars to perform at work, would your existing work ethic and effort deserve that? Million-dollar work ethic is punctual, which means being early and prepared for your start time. Million-dollar work ethic is pleasant and energetic. It's going the extra mile, picking up the slack of others, and encouraging and teaching fellow employees to increase your value and sense of accomplishment. Being an expert at work offers your employer a lot, but doing your best is more important and gives you a sense of accomplishment. Show up early. Work like you're being paid a million dollars. Grind even when no one's watching.

I worked in the first Subway restaurant I owned for seven years, and it was brutal. All I did day in and day out was work in the store. The lack of sales made my results look awful. I was so broke that I couldn't even afford a new "Hours" sign for the front door. I worked ninety-one hours per week for almost twenty months, taking sixty minutes between 3:00 p.m. and 4:00 p.m. to run home and take my dog out or go business to business trying to drum up customers. I worked night shifts alone half the time because I couldn't afford to pay other workers, and when I eventually landed an enormous catering order, I came in at 4:00 a.m. to bake and make more than 200 subs on my own in hopes of finally making a profit. In those early months and years, tight months led to bounced checks. My stress and self-doubt were constant.

Eventually, though, after paying off my debt for that location, I was able to acquire another loan to purchase two more locations. The influx of cash and increase in workload actually benefited me. I was able to do more, work with more flexibility, and address the needs of my restaurants. But don't confuse my opportunity with ease. I worked even harder to oversee, manage, and operate three locations. But that also allowed me to prove to myself and the brand what I could do.

One year after going from one to three locations, Subway of North Carolina voted me the 2019 Operator of the Year. My work ethic didn't change. I had worked my first location so well and so hard for seven years that my work ethic and output became second nature. It is what allowed me to triple my operation and execute. I had been preparing for this for seven years with no accolades, no help, and no attention from the outside world. As a business owner, I didn't have a boss to tell me I was doing a good job or recognize the late nights, early mornings, and effort I poured into the work. There was no annual review or bonus for perseverance. But even without applause, the drive remained. It was instilled in me long before I ever stepped into that role.

My mother learned the value of hard work from her grandfather, a farmer who understood that success wasn't about luck but about showing up every single day, regardless of weather, weariness, or obstacles. For him, the land demanded everything, and he gave it everything in return. That same spirit passed down to my mom who carried it into her own work and life. She taught me that consistent effort is its own kind of reward. My mother graduated *summa cum laude* from college, but she was willing to work day labor for almost six months while she waited to land her first professional job in her field. She was never too good for a job, and she walked that talk.

My father brought with him unshakable grit, earning every dollar with sweat, sacrifice, and pride. He worked long hours, sometimes clocking twenty hours of overtime in one week, chasing bonuses not just for the extra pay but for the dignity that came with pushing beyond what was expected. My parents never assumed anything would be handed to them. They earned every inch of progress.

That work ethic that was born in the fields, sharpened in the hustle of long hours and high expectations, was poured into me from the beginning. And though no one's standing over my shoulder now, that legacy pushes me forward. It's not just about work. It's about honor, endurance, and building something that lasts. That all translates into ability. What I endured was thankless, but once opportunity arose, I was ready to step in and grind it out again, this time in an arena that allowed for visible success. Had I changed? Not in the least. But when life afforded me the opportunity to succeed, I had taken the necessary steps to be prepared. You're not just working for today's reward. You're preparing for tomorrow's opportunity.

What is the lesson?

Joy comes when you realize you didn't waste the waiting but grew stronger because of it. We shouldn't work only for what we have. We need to work toward what we want to have and where

> *Joy comes when you realize you didn't waste the waiting but grew stronger because of it.*

we want to be. We must find purpose and joy in the journey so when life provides us a chance, we are prepared and capable. We haven't wasted so much of our time and opportunity for growth that we are left unprepared and incapable. Take joy in the grind today to be prepared for the joy in succeeding when you get your shot. Every day is another chance to grow, learn, and prepare. Work like you're making a million dollars today so you can be prepared to take advantage tomorrow. It's not about talent. It's about mindset. It's about being steadfast in your values with diligence, vigilance, and commitment, no matter what others are doing around you.

So how *would* you work if you were getting paid a million dollars to teach, to drive, to clean, to build? Would you show up early? Would you be pleasant, diligent, and energized? To those who grind—not occasionally, not when it's convenient, but every single day—this is for you. You don't need a spotlight. You're not chasing applause. You wake up and get after it because it's who you are. Whether people notice or not, whether you get credit or not, you carry yourself with pride because you know what you bring to the table. You know that greatness doesn't come from shortcuts. It comes from discipline, from showing up when no one's watching, and from doing the hard things even when they don't immediately pay off.

If that's you—if you've been giving your best every minute of every day—don't dare stop now. The world might not see your progress yet. You might not have the outcomes you're hoping for yet. But the seeds you're planting are deep, and the roots are growing strong. Keep going. The grind is not just shaping your results; it's shaping you. It's making you stronger, more resilient, and more focused. This kind of ethic doesn't produce weak fruit. It builds legacy, even if that legacy takes time to bloom.

I know this firsthand. Over the last fourteen years, I've poured my mental, emotional, spiritual, and physical self into my work. And if someone looked only at my bank account, they might not see what they'd expect after that kind of effort. Financial freedom still hasn't been the outcome. And that's the truth most people won't say out loud. But here's what I do have. I've earned the freedom to spend time with my children. I've bought flexibility with sweat equity. That, to me, is wealth. That, to me, is worth it. I know exactly what I'm working for, and it's not just money. It's time. Time with my family and time with the people I love.

So to the warriors grinding for glory, I see you. I'm with you. And I'm telling you right now, do not quit. Don't slow down because the world hasn't handed you a trophy yet. Keep your standards high. Keep your ethics Unshaken because quitting only moves you in the wrong direction, away from your goals and, worse, away from your *why*. The next chapters will guide you through how to stay in it for the long haul and how to navigate the seasons where results don't match the effort. Trust me. Patience is part of the payoff.

Stay locked in. Keep showing up. Keep grinding. You're not just working for today's reward; you're building something eternal. Glory isn't given. It's earned. And you are earning it in silence. You're not behind. You're in the middle of becoming everything you were born to be. Keep reading. The best is still ahead.

Practical Steps to a Steadfast Work Ethic

1. *Adopt a Million-Dollar Mindset*
   Work every job, no matter how small, as if it's the opportunity of a lifetime. When you treat each responsibility with intentionality and excellence, doors you never expected can begin to open. A steadfast work ethic starts in the mind. How you see the work in front of you often determines the value you get from it. Even if it's not your dream job, showing up with excellence builds habits and character that will serve you when that dream becomes reality.

2. *Take Joy in the Preparation*
   The world rarely sees the late nights, early mornings, or small, quiet steps forward. But the moments of preparation are the constructs where greatness is built. If you can learn to find joy in the process, in getting a little

better, mastering a detail, or simply showing up again, you'll discover a deep satisfaction that goes beyond external rewards. Trust that the unseen grind is never wasted. It's an investment in your future self.

3. *Celebrate Growth, Not Just Outcomes*
   It's easy to fixate on results such as promotions, accolades, or success milestones. But real joy and resilience come from recognizing your growth along the way. Progress, no matter how incremental, is worth celebrating. When you focus on how far you've come rather than how far you have to go, you fuel your journey with encouragement instead of exhaustion. Growth-centered thinking cultivates endurance and keeps your heart engaged.

4. *Embrace Consistency over Intensity*
   Success doesn't usually come from dramatic bursts of effort but from quiet, consistent action repeated over time. You don't have to be extraordinary every day—just faithful. When you show up even when it's hard, you prove to yourself that you're trustworthy with your own goals. That's where confidence is built, not in perfection but in your ability to keep going.

5. *Align Work with a Greater Purpose*
   When your work is connected to a deeper *why*, it becomes more than a to-do list. It becomes a calling. Even in difficult seasons, remembering who you're doing it for or what it contributes to in the bigger picture can reignite passion and perseverance. Whether it's to provide for your family, serve a cause, or become the

person you were created to be, that purpose can carry you through the toughest days. Purpose breathes life into discipline, turning obligation into opportunity.

Grind today with hope. Persevere today with joy. Prepare today with faith. The opportunity is coming. Reflect and be ready.

Chapter 8

VALUE 2: CHOOSE TOMORROW OVER TODAY

I previously mentioned that my father's family moved from Puerto Rico and that my mother was a farmer's daughter. Coincidentally, while they both lived very different lives, they also lived rather similarly. While Puerto Rico is part of the United States, my father and his parents only spoke Spanish. For all intents and purposes, they lived as immigrants in the giant US city of Chicago. They experienced racism and classism, and they were poor. My mother was a white woman growing up in rural Minnesota. Her father worked the land for decades, growing potatoes and harvesting wheat, driving across the country to sell produce from Minnesota through the Dakotas and down to Kansas.

What was the similarity between the two of them and how they lived? Both were unfortunately poor. Food stamps and government aid helped them and their families survive. The result when they had me was that some of those ways of living were still engrained in their everyday life. Both had good jobs, but the feeling and way of life of having very little persisted. The idea of waste, for example, was unimaginable.

At the age of forty, my father was forced to start over. Addiction to drugs and alcohol led to losing his wife, family, and job. He was forced to move in with his mother and sleep on her couch as he sought after sobriety and a new career. After one year of sobriety and a new career in sales, my father was able to move into a one-bedroom apartment. After achieving both sobriety and his own place to live, my mom allowed my brother and I to stay with him two days a week. Our living accommodations were modest, but that didn't bother him, at least not externally.

I have to believe that his childhood experience of being without is what allowed his existing circumstances to not be life-ruining. In my experience, those who grow up with struggle have greater resilience in adulthood. And I believe that between his life experience and love for us, he was able to focus on what mattered to him—keeping a roof over our heads and food in our tummies. He was willing and able to sacrifice to give us a "normal" life. He was willing to eat cornflakes for dinner for weeks to afford the ridiculously expensive basketball shoes I wanted. We ate rice with ketchup and hot dogs on Wonder Bread at times.

For a couple years, my dad, my brother, and I all shared one queen-sized bed. Honestly, those were some of the funniest times of my life. We would fall asleep crying from laughter. No complaints. No embarrassment. No shame. We just did what was necessary. While that was our life for a few years, I never went without. We had food every night and clothes on our backs, and we lived our lives.

When your circumstances don't carry so much weight that they oppress you, you can still find joy. If what you have matters more to you than who you are or who you have, things that are out of your control will have supreme power over your heart, your mind, your thoughts, and your self-worth. It puts possessions and comfort at the helm of your life. All those things can be stripped away. But if your heart is anchored in relationships of value and you are focused on the journey and your future goals, you can find joy in the difficulties of your walk toward those things.

Fast forward to my first years of business ownership. My father passed away from cirrhosis of the liver that turned into cancer, and I inherited $41,000 in life insurance from him. Talk about guilt. But that money is what I used as a down payment to acquire two very aggressive loans in order to purchase my first Subway restaurant. It was everything I had.

After doing so, my dog Barkley and I moved to the small, rural town where my first location was located. I rented a converted attic in an old country house. The move-in was unreal. The staircase leading to the attic was so small that a queen-size bed frame could not make its way up the stairs. The roof was pitched. There was no central heating or air. I received two "rooms," cable, and Internet for the whopping price of $400 per month. The low cost made me feel safe, but the accommodations, not so much.

My cousin helped me move in. We folded the queen-size mattress the best we could and shoved it up and through the staircase. We placed the dresser along the wall and discovered that the floor was so bowed that the drawers slid open. We tried another wall. Same thing. Eventually I was relegated to placing the dresser at the top of the stairs since that was the flattest floor. I routinely heard squirrels running behind the newly applied drywall, driving me and my dog Barkley nuts. On winter mornings, I would wake up and exhale, able to see my breath. I slept on a mattress on the floor. Creature comforts were nonexistent. My life and the expectations for my life were a far cry from what I hoped they would be. In my mind, this was incredibly temporary. I was wrong.

It took only two months to realize that turning around the restaurant would require more than I had anticipated. I had a belief that my presence would generate a quick turnaround. I assumed that I'd improve the store and its operations so well that I would be profitable after thirty days. I learned that a business owner should never make assumptions but instead analyze what life and the business would be like if nothing changed. That is a lesson of experience that I often teach other business owners.

I worked from open to close with a one-hour break from 3:00 p.m. to 4:00 p.m., seven days a week. I arrived at 7:30 a.m. and left at 10:30 p.m., week after week. At times I had to work the restaurant alone because I couldn't afford the payroll. I had expanded my hours of operation to get every dollar I could, knowing that if I worked those hours myself it wouldn't increase my payroll cost. I would go business to business trying to introduce myself to local businesses and organizations. I grinded daily. That took up almost twenty months of my life.

My body aged significantly. I'm sure that working ninety-one hours per week and sleeping on a mattress on the floor are what generated my lasting foot and back pains. The stress of bouncing checks, making my loan payments, and not having time to mentally and emotionally recover was awful. And what did I get in return for my effort and persistence? In my first year of business, I lost $18,000. I was poor, and after those twelve months, I was facing bankruptcy. No amount of labor or time was going to get me out of this hole. I was a business owner and a son who was petrified of squandering my father's inheritance. Without my mother stepping in and writing the company a check to refinance the debt, I would have lost it all. An additional $43,000 from my mother saved my company and saved me from failure. Unfortunately, it did not change the trajectory or effort the business demanded, but I had survived to fight another day, and then a month, and then a year. I refused to let that define me or minimize the effort I was putting in. I refused to quit. I refused to give in to doubt. I refused to look at my circumstances and expect that I should have more. I was poor, not dead. It was humbling and scary but not insurmountable. My parents' experiences combined with my own taught me what matters. To know their struggles and see them both come out on the other side with successful, happy, fulfilled lives told me that I could, in fact, do the same.

I would be remiss if I neglected the fact that not everyone was raised the same way that I or my parents were. Many people have grown up in households that have the means to obtain creature comforts and life's conveniences. I have learned that all things can be good. We are not expected to live as martyrs, purposefully restricting ourselves from all things material. A beautiful painting, an outfit, a new handbag, or a brand-new toy can be good. The perfectly cooked meal, a beautiful and powerful vehicle, and a home are all worthy pursuits and opportunities to celebrate life's goodness. But beware of seeking material possessions as the *why* you pursue and take joy in. Consider the way others live outside your neighborhood, school, home, and even country. If you have been blessed to not have to live poor, celebrate and appreciate that. But I would challenge you even more to put yourself in situations and places to get a different perspective. Volunteer at homeless shelters or consider temporary foster care. Take mission trips to other parts of the country or other countries. And parents? Take your children. The earlier that perspective enters their minds and souls, the better.

It is those experiences that now shape my wife's and my considerations for our children. Every parent wants to give their children a life better than theirs. But when difficulty and struggle play such a big role in building the grit, inner strength, and determination, and your children have zero experience in those same struggles, what are we to do? How do you teach resilience when the creature comforts of life are all but guaranteed? First, I accept the fact that my kids will not know what it is to be concerned over their parents' ability to pay the rent or stock the fridge. I thank God for those facts every Saturday that we go grocery shopping. But that also means we have to be more proactive in what we allow them to have, do, and experience. They're required to do chores and do them to the satisfaction of "their boss."

Encourage your children to find ways to give back that feel meaningful and accessible to them. They might volunteer at school, help a teacher, or purposely seek out a friend or classmate who seems to need a little extra joy or kindness. Sometimes the smallest acts like sharing a smile, offering a listening ear, or helping carry books can make a profound difference. It's important to be open with your children about the blessings they have and gently encourage them to consider the lives of others, fostering empathy and compassion in their hearts.

My wife and I sponsor a number of children through a global organization called Compassion International. That organization partners with churches in struggling communities around the world, working to improve the lives of children who face tremendous hardships such as living in single-parent homes, being raised in thatch-roofed houses without clean drinking water, and not having medical care or adequate clothing. Writing letters to these children, learning about their lives, praying for them, and sharing their stories with our own kids have been invaluable ways to build perspective and deepen empathy in our family.

Giving back doesn't have to be far away or complicated in order to be impactful. Local opportunities like helping out at a community food pantry, cleaning up a neighborhood park, visiting a nursing home, or supporting a local shelter can have immediate and tangible effects. Those actions teach our children that generosity and gratitude are not just abstract ideas but living practices that enrich our own lives as much as those we help.

Through these experiences, children learn gratitude, not only for the things they have but for the ability to make a positive difference in the world around them. Gratitude, after all, is a practice we all can cultivate, and it is a gift that shapes character, broadens perspectives, and builds hearts that are open and ready to serve.

Sacrifice Today to Thrive Tomorrow

In my early years of building a business, one of the greatest lessons I learned, often through trial and error, was how to live with restraint and discipline. When cash flow was limited and the business wasn't yet profitable, the ability to exercise restraint became essential. It wasn't about what I couldn't do; it was about focusing on the bigger picture and preparing for the future. Discipline, especially when it's tied to our greater purpose, can be the source of immense peace and joy, even when the present moment feels challenging.

Living with restraint teaches us the power of delayed gratification. The ability to postpone immediate desires for something greater is a skill that not only shapes our financial future but enriches our emotional and mental well-being.

Take, for example, a hypothetical entrepreneur named Jake who dreams of opening a brick-and-mortar store but currently runs an online business. Each month, Jake sets aside a portion of his earnings that he could easily spend on personal luxuries such as designer clothes, expensive dinners, and the newest technology. Instead, he chooses to invest in marketing tools, inventory, and customer service training. Over time, that discipline compounds. Three years later, Jake opens the store debt-free with a loyal customer base and a sustainable business model. Restraint in the short term doesn't diminish joy and certainly doesn't diminish success; it enhances it.

There's strong evidence to support this principle. One of the most famous psychological studies on delayed gratification is the Stanford marshmallow experiment conducted by Walter Mischel in the 1970s. Children who were able to delay gratification—

waiting to receive a second marshmallow instead of eating the first one immediately—were shown in follow-up studies to have better life outcomes, including higher SAT scores, better stress management, and lower rates of addiction.

In a more recent and real-world context, financial studies consistently show that people who practice self-discipline with their money, budgeting, saving, and resisting impulsive spending, tend to have significantly higher net worths over time. According to a study published in the *Journal of Behavioral and Experimental Finance*, financial self-control is one of the strongest predictors of wealth accumulation.

In the early days of my business when every dollar was precious and every decision carried weight. I had to resist the temptation to spend unnecessarily. It wasn't just a financial decision; it was a life philosophy. I knew that the sacrifices I made today would create the freedom and success I longed for in the future. And more than that, it gave me a deep sense of purpose. Hope, after all, doesn't die in the soil of sacrifice. It often grows there.

The beauty of delayed gratification lies in its ability to give us a sense of hope and joy as we work toward something greater. When we are willing to sacrifice less important things today for the promise of something better tomorrow, it doesn't feel like deprivation. It feels like an investment in our dreams. This long-term vision brings peace to the difficult decisions we make.

But before we can invest in our dreams, we must first take the time to identify them, and that process often begins in silence. Earlier, we talked about the value of silence, not just as a pause from the noise of life but as a sacred space where clarity is born.

It is in stillness that we often uncover the anchor of our purpose. Without that deep knowing of why we are pursuing something, sacrifice feels like loss. But when we know our purpose, sacrifice becomes strategic. Silence gives us the margin to ask the hard questions. What do I really want? What legacy do I want to leave? What vision is worth saying no to other things for?

> *But when we know our purpose, sacrifice becomes strategic.*

When our dreams are rooted in purpose, they become powerful enough to guide our decisions and sustain our discipline. The temporary happiness that comes from indulging in the now begins to lose its grip because we've tasted something richer: the joy of building a life aligned with calling and vision. Delaying gratification becomes easier when we've glimpsed the joy set before us. In that way, each act of restraint is not a punishment but a deposit, a conscious investment into the kind of future that brings lasting joy, peace, and impact.

Early in my career, I made personal sacrifices that many wouldn't have considered. While others indulged in luxuries, I chose to live below my means. I purchased a home I could afford, not the one I felt I "deserved" or the bank said I could afford. I limited personal spending and focused on investing in what truly mattered: my family, my business, and my health. By prioritizing the things that aligned with my deeper values, I found peace and satisfaction. That sense of restraint and discipline brought me closer to the life I wanted, a life full of purpose, joy, and fulfillment.

The discipline to work hard and live with restraint doesn't just create financial freedom; it creates freedom in every area of life. Through restraint, I've gained the ability to be more present for my family, prioritize my health and well-being, and find time for the things that truly bring me joy.

Owning a business today allows me the freedom to be at home with my children when they're sick, attend their school field trips, and work from home on some days so I can have lunch and Bible study with my wife. I am able to coach my kids in sports, turn off my phone on Sundays, and prioritize my physical and mental health, all because I made sacrifices in the past. It wasn't always easy, but the freedom I experience now is the reward of years spent building restraint and discipline.

But make no mistake. That freedom came at a cost. I made sacrifices along the way that at times were very difficult for me and my loved ones to accept, sacrifices that a standard 9 to 5 offers. There were years when I had to forgo things like vacations, nicer cars, and other material luxuries to ensure that my family and I were able to live within our means. The first handful of years, I worked long hours, often without the safety net of health insurance. Every day felt like a battle, but the joy I found in knowing that each small sacrifice brought me closer to my goals helped me keep going.

Living with restraint is not something we can do in isolation. Accountability partners play an essential role in helping us stay on track and continue living with discipline. We all have moments of weakness or temptation, times when we're ready to throw in the towel or when immediate desires seem to overshadow our long-term goals. That is when the power of accountability shines.

I've made a point to surround myself with people I trust and respect, people who can hold me accountable when my discipline falters. Whether it's my wife, my mother, or my close friends, I've learned to lean on those individuals to keep me focused on my goals. It's through accountability that I find the strength to stay the course, especially when life feels overwhelming.

One example of this is my commitment to living sober for thirty days multiple times per year to ensure that alcohol doesn't have a controlling influence in my life. I've seen the power of indulgence and substance abuse in my family, and I knew that for my well-being, I needed to take proactive steps to maintain control. Accepting the reality of my human nature—that I can be selfish, indulgent, and prone to immediate gratification—is the first step toward living with discipline. The act of testing and refining my self-control has brought me growth, peace, and ultimately joy.

My mom limited her promotions early in her career because she prioritized being home with us during our formative years. Later, as we grew older, she advanced in her career, eventually becoming the CEO of her company, flying all over the United States and even routinely addressing the United Nations. What that showed me was that true joy comes from knowing why you're making sacrifices. She wasn't sacrificing for the sake of sacrifice; she was sacrificing because her family was her priority. The joy of knowing her *why* made the sacrifices worth it.

Living with restraint and discipline doesn't just change our circumstances; it changes us. It strengthens our character, deepens our resilience, and empowers us to overcome the challenges we will inevitably face. More than that, it gives us a sense of joy that cannot be easily shaken because it's joy born from living in alignment with our deepest values.

My Uncle John was another person in my life who was a great example of discipline. He is the one who got me into Subway in the first place. He owned three restaurants and sought my help managing them back in 2009. Despite his success and financial freedom, Uncle John led a materialistically humble life. He had an entertainment center that he made himself out of plywood and cardboard (I am dead serious) and a car that felt less stable on the highway than a go-kart would have. Granted, that was his kids' car, but still, he refused to splurge! That afforded him financial peace and freedom. By limiting his spending and expenses, he was able to pay many things in cash over credit and typically without loans. He also taught me discipline when it came to diving into my faith. We need to set aside time every day to dive into and anchor into what we believe. That requires discipline among the demands on our time by any and all things worldly.

Restraint and discipline are not burdens. They are the gateways to a life of true joy and fulfillment. They are the tools we use to shape a life that is aligned with our deepest values and create a future we can be proud of. Through restraint, we learn to appreciate the things that truly matter. We find strength on the journey and experience a deep, abiding joy that can never be taken away.

That doesn't mean it's easy. It doesn't mean we never falter. But it does mean that every step forward, no matter how small, is a step in the right direction, and that is something to celebrate.

Practical Steps

1. *Start with Perspective*

   Begin by shifting your mindset. True discipline starts not with denial but with gratitude. Look at what you have through the lens of perspective. Remember that someone else is carrying heavier burdens or making do with far less. When you see your life as a blessing, even the practice of restraint feels like a privilege, not punishment. Someone will always have more. A bigger house. A newer car. A shinier job title. But joy anchored in material things will always drift. Choose contentment, not comparison.

2. *Connect Discipline to Purpose*

   Restraint makes sense when it serves something greater. Ask yourself, *What kind of life am I building? What kind of legacy am I leaving?* When you see the *why* behind your discipline, the *how* becomes far more sustainable.

3. *Audit Your Habits, Especially Your Spending*

   Your bank account can be a spiritual journal. It shows what you value most. Organize your expenses from largest to smallest. Ask yourself, *Does this reflect the kind of person I want to be?* If not, take the first small step toward change. "For where your treasure is, there your heart will be also" (Matt. 6:21).

4. *Save with Intention*

   Saving money isn't just smart financial advice; it's a mindset of discipline and intention. It says, *I believe thoughtful planning leads to greater outcomes than acting on impulse.* Whether you're running a business or just getting started, save something. Anything. Make it a habit, not an afterthought. And if you've hit rock bottom financially or otherwise, remember, there's still hope. Even in mom's basement at the age of forty, you aren't finished.

5. *Build Boundaries, Not Barriers*
Discipline is not about self-punishment. It's about self-protection. Boundaries around spending, time, energy, and emotions help preserve peace and prevent burnout. For example, paying your rent or mortgage every month would be most people's first priority. Eating out or spending money on nonessential things would be lower on the list. A boundary would be to not touch the money designated for your home.

6. *Be Consistent, Not Perfect*
You'll slip. Everyone does. Discipline isn't about flawless performance. It's about faithful return. Show up again. Reset. Refocus. Restart. There's grace for every stumble and growth in every step.

7. *Celebrate Small Wins*
Did you save some money this month? Did you decline that unnecessary purchase? Did you wake up early for prayer or reflection? Celebrate that. Every small step is evidence that you're building a life of meaning, not just managing a schedule.

Every small choice matters. Whether it's saving a small amount or choosing to live simply, discipline in the "little things" prepares us for greater responsibility and blessing.

Chapter 9

VALUE 3: GROW THROUGH THE WAIT

In a world that glorifies immediacy—instant success, quick results, overnight transformations—patience has almost become a forgotten virtue. But for anyone truly chasing something real, something lasting, or something meaningful, patience isn't optional. It is essential.

To live an Unshaken life means to walk through seasons of uncertainty without letting them derail your identity. It means holding onto your *why* with both hands, even when the world gives you every reason to let go. And it means believing, even in the silence, that what you're doing and who you're becoming are not in vain.

Patience is often labeled a virtue, a noble ideal that sounds

> *To live an Unshaken life means to walk through seasons of uncertainty without letting them derail your identity. It means holding onto your why with both hands, even when the world gives you every reason to let go. And it means believing, even in the silence, that what you're doing and who you're becoming are not in vain.*

nice in theory but feels impossible when your plans fall apart and life leaves you in limbo. But for those who strive to live Unshaken, patience is more than just a passive posture. It is a powerful act of hope. It is an intentional discipline rooted in the belief that every delay, every detour, every moment of waiting is not wasted. It's preparing.

At Become Unshaken, we believe a joyful and hope-filled life doesn't ignore hardship. It stares it down, breathes through it, and waits with purpose. Living unshaken means trusting that the timing of your life, even when it feels off, is still part of something greater. You may not understand it in the moment, but hope whispers, *This delay is not your denial.*

There was a time when waiting felt like torture—an interruption to my plans, a threat to my sense of control. I was fiery, quick to speak, quicker to react. My Puerto Rican Viking blood ran hot, and I expected the world to move at my pace. If things didn't happen when I thought they should, I spiraled into frustration. It may have been dressed up as passion, but deep down, I knew it was impatience dressed up in intensity.

The waiting seasons—those long stretches of silence and uncertainty, of forced delay out of my control, began to chip away at me. At first, I fought them. I demanded clarity and pushed against the slowness like a bull in a cage. But the more I resisted, the more I realized I wasn't just waiting for an outcome; I was being reshaped in the process.

Over time, something changed. The fire didn't leave, but it learned to simmer instead of scorch. I began to understand that not everything and not everyone was meant to operate on my schedule. What once made me unbearably demanding now led me toward understanding and empathy. I listened more. I judged less. My once-irritable spirit found tranquility and peace.

Waiting taught me to surrender control without losing my strength. It didn't weaken me; it refined me. I became anchored, not because the storms stopped but because I stopped needing to control the wind. And in that sacred stillness, I found a version of myself I never would have met if life had always moved at my pace. But let me be honest. This is still the principle I struggle with most. Patience doesn't come naturally to me, and even now, I often feel that pull to charge ahead, to solve, to fix, and to conquer.

The desire to push forward and attack every obstacle head on hasn't disappeared. It lingers, and I have to choose daily to remember what waiting has already taught me. I have to remind myself of the blessings that came through delayed answers, closed doors, and seasons of stillness. I'm learning that patience is a posture of trust. So I actively pursue it, not because it's easy but because it's necessary. It anchors me. It transforms me. And it draws me closer to the heart of peace that is never in a rush but always right on time. You see, patience wasn't just waiting. It's who I became while I waited that mattered.

When you live Unshaken, patience becomes an act of faith. It becomes the ground where hope grows. It turns frustration into fuel and delay into development. Joy isn't found in the speed of the journey. It's found in the strength built along the way. Hope doesn't erase hardship, but it gives you a reason to keep going when you don't yet see the outcome. Patience teaches you to embrace the unseen, find peace in progress, and hold onto your purpose even when your path looks different than expected.

So if you find yourself in a season of uncertainty, if the doors won't open and the timeline feels off, if you're living at home when you thought you'd be on your own, if your current role feels beneath your capabilities or disconnected from your dream, take heart. You are not forgotten. You are being forged. Keep going. Keep choosing hope. Keep choosing joy. Let the trials refine you, not define you. Remember, the delays are not in vain. They are preparing you for something far greater than what you imagined. And one day, when you look back, you'll see it clearly. The patience that felt like punishment was actually the birthplace of your greatest strength.

Be patient and trust that even in the waiting, joy is possible. Hope is alive, and your purpose is unfolding. Patience stretches you. It refines your reactions, reveals your deepest motivations, and demands maturity. When your goals don't come easily, you learn discipline. When people misunderstand you, you learn grace. When doors don't open, you learn trust. And when you feel stuck, you learn stillness.

That kind of character, rooted in perseverance, humility, and hope, is the kind of strength that sustains success once it arrives. Because if you get what you want before you've become the person who can handle it, it'll crush you. Patience ensures that you grow at the pace your purpose demands. And in that process, however long it takes, joy is still possible.

> *That kind of character, rooted in perseverance, humility, and hope, is the kind of strength that sustains success once it arrives.*

Our ability to remain steadfast is deeply tied to our sense of purpose and faith in what we are doing. When we align our principles with a higher purpose—whether our faith, our mission, or our personal vision—we find the strength to keep moving forward, even in the face of uncertainty.

Our faith and trust in this belief provide the hope that no matter what challenges we face, we are ultimately working toward something greater. That hope fuels our perseverance and brings us joy, knowing that our efforts are not in vain. It allows us to endure the hardest of times, confident that our commitment to our values will lead to lasting success and fulfillment. A patient heart is marked by hope and quiet joy, even in the midst of uncertainty. It is a posture of trust, believing that though we may not see the full picture now, all things are working together for good. In contrast, an impatient heart becomes restless and frustrated, often allowing bitterness and anxiety to seep into every corner of life. Impatience, if left unchecked, can sabotage not only our progress but our peace, robbing us of the beauty that comes from trusting the process.

Remaining steadfast in our values is not always the easiest path, but it is the one that leads to the deepest, most lasting joy. Choosing patience is ultimately an act of faith, believing that what we build slowly with integrity and trust will stand the test of time. The journey may be long and the obstacles may seem insurmountable, but as we choose to stay true to our values, even when no one is watching, we are sowing the seeds for a future filled with fulfillment, purpose, and joy. Success isn't about instant gratification. It's about the long, steady journey of staying true to what we believe in, every single day. And that, my friends, is where true joy and lasting hope are found.

Practical Steps

1. *Start with Trust, Not Timelines*

   Patience begins by letting go of the need to control the timing of everything. Think about waiting for a job offer after an interview. You've done everything you can. You've prepared, showed up, and followed up. And now the outcome is out of your hands. Obsessing over the timing doesn't speed it up; it only drains your energy. Trust allows you to stay grounded while things unfold. When you feel anxious about when something will happen, shift your focus to how you're waiting. Practice daily moments of release such as going for a walk, talking it out with a friend, or journaling your thoughts. Remind yourself that some of the best opportunities take time to develop behind the scenes.

2. *Choose Surrender over Striving*

   In moments of impatience, we often try to force outcomes. But surrender isn't giving up. It's choosing inner calm while staying committed. Think of Nelson Mandela, activist and former President of South Africa. He waited twenty-seven years in prison without bitterness. Practice stillness. Turn off distractions, rest in a favorite chair, or simply breathe deeply for sixty seconds. Surrender isn't weakness. It's wise restraint in the face of urgency.

   "He who has a why to live for can bear almost any how." —Friedrich Nietzsche

3. *Focus on What You Can Do Today*

   When we live too far in the future, anxiety grows. Patience strengthens when we give energy to what's in front of us. Each morning, choose one small, meaningful task that moves you forward. Whether it's learning, connecting, or taking a healthy step, progress lives in the present.

4. *Celebrate Small Progress*

   Progress is rarely loud or dramatic. It's slow, subtle, and often invisible at first. Think of Michelangelo who said, "Every block of stone has a statue inside it." He carved patiently, knowing that beauty takes time. Kurt Vonnegut once said, "Enjoy the little things in life because one day you'll look back and realize they were the big things." That mindset is essential when our progress feels too quiet to matter. Every small step forward is part of a greater transformation. Keep a journal or notes app. Write down tiny wins like a shift in mindset, a meaningful conversation, or a task completed. Celebrating small things makes big things feel possible.

5. *Surround Yourself with Encouragement*

   Impatience grows in isolation. Surrounding yourself with people who have endured tough seasons and came through stronger can reframe your perspective. Think of teams training together. Resilience spreads in community. Find mentors, peers, or even authors and thinkers whose stories encourage you. Join a group, read biographies, or listen to podcasts that fuel your endurance. I'd suggest the Become Unshaken podcast, but that's just me.

6. *Speak Life While You Wait*

Language shapes mindset. Neuroscience even shows that positive self-talk can regulate emotion and reduce stress. Ancient wisdom from many traditions reminds us that words have power. Catch negative thoughts. Replace them with affirmations like these: "This season is shaping me. Growth is happening, even if I can't see it." What you say to yourself during waiting becomes your inner soundtrack.

7. *Remember What You're Waiting For*

Whether it's a personal goal, a career dream, or healing, remembering your *why* helps you endure the *when*. Think of Thomas Edison, who said, "I have not failed. I've just found 10,000 ways that won't work." Write down your vision or goal. Post it somewhere visible. Revisit it regularly, not to demand speed but to stay connected to your hope.

Patience is powerful. It leads to joy that isn't based on circumstances and hope that grows deeper even in delay.

Chapter 10

VALUE 4: FALL. RISE. REPEAT.

There are mornings when the weight of the world feels like too much to carry. There are days when the news is bad, the bank account is low, and the silence of unanswered prayers echo loudly. Life guarantees it. Storms will come, and sometimes they hit harder than we ever imagined. We lose jobs, friendships falter, dreams crumble, and the unexpected knocks us flat. But here's the truth that steadies us. The ground may shake, but we don't have to stay down.

You may not have power over the waves that hit, but you hold the power to rise. Every single day, no matter how weary you feel or how long the night has been, you have the sacred choice to get up. It's not about feeling ready. It's not about having everything figured out. Rising is an act of courage; a decision made before the breakthrough comes.

> *Every single day, no matter how weary you feel or how long the night has been, you have the sacred choice to get up.*

Scripture tells us that God's mercies are new every morning, not because life gets easier but because God gives strength for each step. Joy may seem distant at first, but it is often found in the act of moving forward, even when hope feels like a whisper. Getting up doesn't mean the pain disappears or the battle is over. It means you are refusing to let the struggle define your story. It means that even with tears in your eyes and questions in your heart, you are choosing to lean into a deeper promise that you are not alone and that perseverance brings a harvest, even if you can't see it yet.

There is a quiet, sacred power in simply getting up, especially when life has knocked you down with the full weight of sorrow, disappointment, or uncertainty. Rising after a loss, after failure, or in the face of grief is not a denial of pain. It's a testament to purpose. I learned this not from easy moments but from the most soul-wrenching seasons of my life when love and loss collided in deeply personal, irreversible ways. In those times, I discovered that getting up isn't about feeling strong. It's about choosing to rise again and again because your purpose still calls and your story still matters.

I was living in North Carolina, steadily preparing to build a business from the ground up—something my father deeply believed in and wanted for me. Back in Chicago, he was fighting a losing battle with liver cancer. It was a brutal reality that hung like a quiet weight over everything I did. He was proud of my work and told me often that I was doing the right thing by staying the course, even as disease slowly claimed his body. Our last visit was a joyful one. He came to North Carolina for my younger brother Joseph's Marine Corps graduation. None of us said it, but we all felt the nearing end. After that visit, we talked even more often, spoke more vulnerably, and loved more openly. The ticking clock gave our conversations a kind of beauty that comes only when time is scarce. There was a quiet strength in his acceptance and in mine, a strength that didn't shout but whispered *keep going.*

When he passed, it shattered me. Our almost daily phone calls were no more. It would be years before my inclination to call about my day or tell him a funny story would stop. But I got up, not because the grief was gone but because he would have wanted that. My path was never meant to stop in the valley. I pushed forward, building with diligence, not just for me but in honor of the love we shared and the dreams and pride he had for me. I carried that strength into every deal, every success, and every challenge. His encouraging voice still echoes in my heart, not as a ghost but as a guide.

Then came the sudden loss of my uncle, the man who stepped into my life like a second father after mine passed. His heart attack was swift, jarring, and entirely without warning. Unlike the gradual goodbye I had with my dad, there was no preparation, no farewell call, and no final moment of connection. There was just silence where his voice used to be. The shock of it nearly buckled me. But again, I chose to get up, not out of obligation but from a place of deep resolve. I live this life for them. Their sacrifices, their strength, their belief in me. None of it will be in vain.

Getting up doesn't always look heroic. Sometimes it's just getting out of bed. Sometimes it's making that phone call, showing up to work, or choosing to smile when your heart is heavy. But every time I rise, I do so anchored in the legacy of two parents and an uncle who helped shape me. I get up because life is still worth living, because purpose is still alive in me, and because an Unshaken life is not one without sorrow but one that stands firm in the face of it.

> *I get up because life is still worth living, because purpose is still alive in me, and because an Unshaken life is not one without sorrow but one that stands firm in the face of it.*

Today, as you face whatever stands in your way, remember that victory doesn't always look like a grand finish. Sometimes it looks like simply standing back up. And in that moment, heaven leans in, and strength is renewed.

So make that choice today. Choose to get up.

You Will Lose

The latest youth basketball season was incredible. One of my kids' teams had a 7-1 record and scored the most points in the entire league. We were one of the favorites to win it all. In our first game of the playoffs against a team with drastically worse statistics, we were absolutely dominated from start to finish. Our team and I were shocked. Absolutely nothing went our way. So here I was with a bunch of little humans looking to me for answers, and what was my response to them? There is only one champion. Everyone else loses. I believe that is a lesson we all often lie about to ourselves and to others. It's a lesson we easily forget. You play to win the game. But in every game, there is also a loser.

Success is hard-earned and a long journey. There are very few fast roads to success. Most people fail over and over again, learning from losses in pursuit of victory and success. The list of my losses feels endless, despite the present, external appearance of success so many would argue that I have. In many ways, I lost my childhood at a young age. A family turned upside down by substance abuse led me to take on the mindset and role of an adult at much too young of an age. I lost when I obtained the career I had so desperately wanted and then discovered that it was, in fact, the last thing I was meant to do.

I lost my father to cancer. Right before I purchased my first restaurant, almost every material possession I had was stolen from a storage unit, including mementos from my father's funeral and the American flag the U.S. Army gave my grandfather for his service when he passed. I lost seven years of my life and aged double that amount after the ninety-one-hour workweeks I put in when I bought my first restaurant. My first marriage failed, making me absent from my children's lives half a week, every week. My uncle unexpectedly passed from a heart attack. There is simply no escaping the reality of loss in this life.

But losing creates perseverance. Losing builds character. Losing strengthens a person's resolve and ability to overcome hardship. And it is necessary because losses are everywhere. The stock market crashes, an investor pulls out, or a natural disaster sweeps your business away. A loved one passes, you fail an exam, or you start your career over at the age of fifty. How will you respond? Will you quit? Are you of the mindset that something is owed to you? Or do you lace up your sneakers the next day and work on your game? We all lose. But will you quit, or will you grind it out for the future win?

Life Isn't Fair, So Choose to Get Up Anyway

As a father of six, I hear the complaint of "that isn't fair" almost daily. And as a parent, I know there is a fine line between teaching lessons that are difficult to accept and sounding calloused. But when it comes to fair, I rarely mince words, especially with the big boys. I tell them, "Life isn't fair, so now what?" You see, I can't allow my kids to be paralyzed by not being treated equally. "Life isn't fair" isn't just something we say when a child loses a toy or a turn. It's a brutal, historical truth backed by generations of evidence.

We live in a world where movements like Black Lives Matter exist not because things are equal but because systemic injustice still shapes our daily lives. Innocent people are wrongfully deported even when they were born on American soil, simply because of their last name or skin color. In neighborhoods across the country, kids grow up dodging violence instead of chasing dreams, and their zip code dictates the quality of their schools, food, and futures. Some people will start three laps ahead in a race you didn't even know had begun. That's reality.

More simplistically, they might not get picked first on the playground or passed the ball in a game. They may get a C when they thought they earned an A. Their sibling might not clean up the playroom as well as they do. Heck, sometimes they have to clean up messes that aren't theirs. Why? Because life isn't fair, and a job still needs to get done.

How do you respond when things aren't fair? Is shutting it down and walking away an option? If your kiddo isn't the first pick at dodgeball, do you step in, or do you encourage them to push on, step up, and march on? If their teacher gives them a C, are you emailing the teacher to get the grade changed or diving in with your kiddo on how to improve their grade the next time? There are always two responses to a situation. Forward or backward? Fight or flight? Push on or quit? The lesson I try to teach my kids is not to sink into hopelessness or despair but to rise with resolve. Life won't always hand you fairness, so learn to refuse to quit. I don't want my kids to ever give up.

> *Life won't always hand you fairness, so learn to refuse to quit.*

So sometimes things aren't fair. That doesn't mean you can't find another way to obtain what you want. That doesn't mean our goals are impossible to reach. That doesn't mean we have no shot. It simply means we have to work harder, find alternative ways to accomplish our goals, and persevere until we reach those goals. Don't let the world tell you it's impossible. Don't let the unfairness of life get in the way. Stand up, press on, and learn to fight for yourself with integrity, grit, and unshakable hope. Cry and lament as you must, but then get up. Keep getting up. Because while life isn't fair, you were made to overcome anyway. Fairness is not a prerequisite for greatness.

You Aren't Sick Unless You Have a Fever, Are Bleeding, or Puking – Or So I Was Raised

Hands down, my mother is unquestionably the toughest person I have ever known. Her inner strength is enviable. Her mental endurance is unmatched. A lot of my values and the way I live are a direct reflection of how she raised me. As both a parent and a CEO, she never took the easy road to reach her goals, and she never taught me to take it either. In fact, she made it clear that the more difficult road was often the one worth walking. That's where the growth was. That's where the deeper, more meaningful rewards came. She lived it. She worked it. She raised me by it.

Starting at an entry-level position with a national substance abuse corporation, she rose to become its CEO. She met with former presidents of the United States. She addressed the United Nations. And she did all of this as a single mother of two boys in the 1980s and 1990s, often turning down promotions and professional opportunities to be present during our formative years but never taking her foot off the gas. Her shoes were massive. But she gave me the grit, focus, and resilience to walk boldly in them.

Here is one of her infamous rules: "You're not sick unless you're bleeding, puking, or have a fever" (and our thermometer never worked). This was the standard in our home. And back then, it made sense for who we were, what we had, and the times we were in. It was about grit. It was about survival. It was about teaching two boys how to endure when life didn't make endurance easy. I share this not to minimize anyone's experience but to explain mine. The world has changed, and thankfully, so has our awareness. At Become Unshaken, we fully recognize that not all pain is visible. Chronic illness, mental health battles, and emotional exhaustion can be just as debilitating as physical symptoms, and we hold space for that always.

Still, my mother's rule wasn't rooted in insensitivity. It was rooted in discipline and a refusal to let minor discomforts keep us from showing up. In our home, staying home from school wasn't a break. It meant real rest with no screens and no fun meals. Just fluids, books, and stillness. There was a clear message: Unless you're truly unwell, you get up and get going.

That line between what stops us and what we can overcome is one she taught me to identify early. Basketball was my passion. From ages seven to sixteen, it was everything. But if I missed school, I missed the game. Period. I learned to be honest with myself. Was I really sick or just tired? Was it truly illness or just discomfort? Watching Michael Jordan play with the flu didn't help my case either. If he could push through, I could too. And often I did.

That mindset bred in me an unshakable belief in mental strength. It taught me that while I can't always control what's happening in my body, I can decide how I respond. A cold, a headache, a long night of poor sleep—those things never stop me from being a dad, a husband, a business owner, or a coach.

And here's the point. Not every hardship requires us to stop. And not every excuse is a real one. Let me be clear. I'm not talking about denying yourself care when you need it. I'm not talking about ignoring serious illness or pushing through in ways that damage your health. But too often we talk ourselves out of growth because of inconvenience, discomfort, or fear. We create barriers that aren't truly there. This chapter is about questioning that.

Mental toughness doesn't mean denying reality. It means refusing to let lesser things derail greater callings. It means taking stock of your circumstances honestly and deciding what you can still do. Life is full of real pain—grief, sickness, depression, loss. We won't pretend otherwise. But if you can rise today, even in a small way, do it. If it's within you to show up, even if it's imperfect, then show up. Some days your win will be crushing it at work. Some days it will be just getting out of bed. Either way, your mindset matters.

This isn't about ignoring the storm. It's about choosing not to be defined by it. You've done hard things before. You can do hard things again. So get up today. You've got it in you. Now prove it.

Don't Let Fear Paralyze You

Fear is a powerful emotion. It creeps in when we least expect it, whispering doubts, amplifying insecurities, and attempting to stop us from stepping forward. But for some of us, fear didn't whisper. It roared. Don't let fear paralyze you.

Fear is a powerful force, one that often drives our decisions more than we realize. We convince ourselves we're being logical or safe when in reality we're making choices from a place of fear. And when fear is in the driver's seat, it almost always takes us off course.

Some people fear rejection so they don't speak up. They don't apply. They don't ask. They don't reach out. They'd rather stay in their comfort zone than risk the possibility of hearing no. But that comfort zone can quickly become a prison.

Others fear judgment, so they live in a constant loop of second-guessing their instincts, hiding their gifts, or shaping themselves into what they believe others want them to be. They walk on eggshells and apologize for taking up space. And over time, they begin to forget who they even are.

Still others fear being alone. They stay in unhealthy relationships, avoid independence, or try to numb that ache of solitude through distractions or overcommitment. The fear of being unwanted or unseen drives them to cling to the wrong people or fill their calendars to the point of burnout.

Fear, when left unchecked, does not protect us. It prevents us. It holds us back from our calling, our peace, and the very things we were made to pursue. The key is not to eliminate fear completely; it's to refuse to let it lead. Faith, purpose, and identity must be the compass instead.

My first experiences with fear came early. My father, during my formative years, was a man gripped by addiction. That addiction transformed him into someone I didn't recognize, someone I was terrified of. When the most important man in your life becomes the most dangerous, it changes you. It shapes your sense of safety, trust, and love. And it certainly reshapes your perception of fear.

There will never be a man, person, or event scarier to me than an out-of-control father fueled by substances and pain. The very presence of fear lived in our home, and for a long time, I thought fear would define me forever. But it didn't.

You see, what I didn't understand then, but see so clearly now, is that something was still unfolding. Even in the chaos, even in the fear, even in the pain, a story was being written. One that would one day include healing, strength, and, yes, even joy.

Over time, that pain turned into a peculiar sort of power. My childhood fear, once crippling, became the very foundation of the resilience I carry today. The storm I walked through became the reason I no longer tremble when others try to intimidate me. My past helped form an unshaken core that I've leaned on again and again.

Now don't mistake me. That doesn't mean I became hard or unfeeling. It was quite the opposite. It made me more compassionate, more tender, and more intentional about who I wanted to be and how I wanted to love those around me. I had a choice, and so do you. We all carry scars. We all have wounds that haven't quite healed. And we all have the choice to either allow those wounds to define us or refine us. Pain can paralyze, or it can propel.

> *Let me say this as clearly and lovingly as I can. You are not what happened to you. You are not your trauma. You are not the worst day of your life. You are the survivor of it. You are the one who endured it. And you are still here. Still standing. Still capable of joy.*

Let me say this as clearly and lovingly as I can. You are not what happened to you. You are not your trauma. You are not the worst day of your life. You are the survivor of it. You are the one who endured it. And you are still here. Still standing. Still capable of joy.

That's the beauty of a life Unshaken. It doesn't mean untouched. It means unmoved. Grounded. Rooted. For me, that story took a redemptive turn. My father eventually overcame his addictions. By the time I was ten, he had sobered up and made the courageous choice to rebuild what had been broken. My brother, seven years my junior, didn't even know the version of my father I had grown up with and lived with. And to boot, I was given seventeen more years with him. Sober, he was the most loving, demonstrative man I knew. He called me "pumpkin" and kissed my cheek even as I became a young man. He couldn't undo the past, but he refused to let it write the final chapter of his story. And that's what I want to leave with you today. The past may have shaped you, but it doesn't own your future.

As a grown man now and a father to six beautiful children, I take the lessons I learned, both painful and powerful, and teach them with love instead of letting them repeat through pain. My father's legacy, like mine, won't be defined by our worst moments. It will be defined by our response, by our resilience, by our choice to rise.

To anyone who has walked through trauma, especially at the hands of those who were supposed to protect you, my heart is with you. My prayers go out for you. If you are in an abusive relationship—whether emotional, physical, or spiritual—get help. Leave. Don't wait for things to magically get better. Choose yourself. Choose life. Choose healing. It's possible. The world can be dark, but darkness cannot overcome the light. And fear cannot paralyze a heart filled with hope and purpose.

So today I say this to you: Stand up not in defiance, but in faith. Not in anger but in strength. You were created for more than just survival. You were created for purpose, for joy, and for love. There is no time for fear because your future is too important. Your calling is too great. Your joy is too precious.

Let your scars remind you not of the pain but of the healing. Let your strength tell the story of how you overcame. And let your life reflect a life that brings beauty from ashes, light from darkness, and courage from fear.

Just Get It Done

When life throws its inevitable curveballs, our natural instinct is often to hesitate. We overthink, we analyze, and we second-guess our next move. But what if the real magic lies in simply showing up? Whether it's apologizing even when you feel justified, holding your peace in a heated moment, or making time for that tough conversation you've been avoiding, the act of stepping forward is transformational.

Hope and joy are not passive emotions. They are cultivated through action. You may feel weak or unsure, but every time you lean into a difficult situation, you build an inner reservoir of strength. It's in the moment you schedule that hard conversation or swallow your pride to make amends that you experience real empowerment.

Showing up doesn't mean you'll get it perfect. You might stumble over your words, feel awkward, or even meet resistance. But being Unshaken tells us that strength is perfected in weakness. Each courageous step, no matter how small, reinforces your resilience and keeps you anchored in hope.

Life won't stop presenting challenges. Hormonal teenagers will test your patience, colleagues will misunderstand you, and friends will hurt your feelings. But remember, you are stronger than the discomfort. Keep showing up. Just do it. The joy is in the journey, not in the perfection of outcomes.

One of the hardest lessons we learn is that we can't control how others respond. We can only control our choices. There's deep freedom in recognizing that the weight of the world isn't on our shoulders; it's in our hands to act but not to dictate results.

Hope thrives in surrender. When you apologize, even when you're right, you aren't giving up your dignity. You're choosing peace over pride. When you hold your tongue with your teenager, you are not being weak. You are modeling grace under pressure.

And when you initiate a tough conversation, you are not risking rejection as much as you are honoring truth.

Just get it done isn't about recklessness or the half-hearted completion of something. It's about courage paired with faith. It's knowing that every challenge is an invitation to grow deeper roots of resilience and experience the quiet joy that comes from acting in love and integrity. You may never win the argument or change someone's mind, but you will win the battle for your own heart.

Joy and hope are fueled by action. Each time you choose to face difficulty head on, you reinforce your Unshaken spirit. Remember, life's struggles don't stop, but neither does your capacity to rise above them. Just get it done, not because it's easy but because it's worth it.

There are moments in life when the only way forward is to simply get up. It's not because the pain has passed or because the weight has lifted but because choosing to rise becomes an act of defiance against everything that's trying to keep you down. I've had to make that decision more times than I can count. Betrayal by people I invested in—people I poured time, trust, and mentorship into—left a deep wound. I've been blindsided by those who walked away. I've watched relationships fracture and experienced the deep sorrow of being misunderstood by those I thought knew my heart.

Each of those moments brought a choice: Stay stuck or just get it done. I made the choice to get up and move forward, not because I had the emotional bandwidth or because the pain had passed but because I had to. I had responsibilities, people who relied on me, and a calling too important to abandon.

Life didn't pause for my pain. I had to get up. I had to press forward because the opportunities to choose grit over giving up are endless in a life that includes real struggle.

Stephanie recalls a particular day when the world seemed to be attacking me from every direction. I was exhausted mentally, physically, emotionally, and spiritually. She could see the hurt in my face. I was losing the battle that week, and I was losing big. And then I made the choice to write my first "personal psalm," a psalm that would tell about every difficult situation God had pulled me out of. Regardless of your beliefs, you can do something similar. It is a grocery list of hardship, pain, and suffering, as well as the victories I had been given. The list was more than three pages long. At the end of every difficult occasion and reminder of victory, I included, "His steadfast love endures forever." Yours may read, "and yet I survived" or some other mantra you can anchor to for future difficulty.

I was restored and reenergized. I was reminded that the week was not the worst of my life and that I had been strengthened and had overcome greater obstacles. Not a single problem from that week ceased, and there are plenty of moments in my life that have yet to be resolved, but I refocused my racing mind on the facts. I had overcome before and could overcome again. It gave me power over the situation and faith that once again I would get through this. So get up, even if it's messy, even if it's slow. There's strength in that first step and in the thousand more that follow. That decision is what fortifies the ground beneath your feet.

This is what it means to live an Unshaken life. It's not a life free of suffering or uncertainty but a life grounded in the unchanging truth that I've been carried before and I'll be carried again. Sometimes the most powerful thing you can do is get up and just get it done, not with perfect confidence but with quiet belief. That one step—again and again—is where strength is forged. That is where peace begins. That is where I remain: Unshaken.

Resilience isn't something we are born with. It's something we build, one choice at a time. Life will knock you down. It will bruise your pride, break your heart, and leave you wondering if it's worth the effort to get up again. But here's the truth. Hope and joy aren't found in avoiding hardship; they're discovered in the act of rising every single time.

Just get it done is a principle woven with threads of faith, hope, and perseverance. When you embrace the mindset of *just get it done*, you learn that action itself is powerful. When fear threatens to paralyze you, you press forward anyway because courage is not the absence of fear; it's moving despite it. And when life's injustices weigh heavily and things don't go your way, you make the bold choice to rise regardless, trusting that your effort has meaning, even if the outcome seems unfair.

The past reminds us that we are not alone in the struggle. Joy teaches us that our peace does not have to be tethered to perfect circumstances. Each day presents a new invitation to stand up, face the challenges, and pursue your purpose with determination. You won't always feel strong, but you are stronger than you think. And the more you do it, the more evidence you have to support your strength to do it again.

Here's a hard but freeing truth we already discussed: You will lose. Plans will fail, relationships may fracture, and outcomes will often disappoint. Life on earth guarantees difficulty and, yes, loss. But loss is not the enemy; fear of it is.

Choosing to get up again isn't about guaranteeing victory. It's about honoring your calling and your capacity to grow. Every setback is a setup for deeper strength and greater grace. You'll face moments when your best effort seems wasted, but in those moments, reminders of survival anchor you. They tell you that the act of rising is never wasted, even when the results aren't what you hoped for.

Hope and joy remain your companions, whispering that the fight is worth it. Resilience is born not in perfect endings but in faithful beginnings. Whether you're facing personal disappointment, relational struggles, or unexpected losses, the choice remains: Get up.

Perseverance isn't glamorous, but it is sacred. And as you keep choosing to rise every day in every situation, you'll find that joy becomes a quiet undercurrent, faith becomes your firm foundation, and hope keeps your heart light, no matter how heavy life feels. That is what it means to live Unshaken.

Practical Steps to Fall. Rise. Repeat. Successfully.

1. *Acknowledge the Fall Without Shame*

   Falling doesn't make you weak. It makes you human. There's no growth in pretending you're fine when you're not. Real strength begins when you admit the setback without drowning in shame. Speak honestly with someone you trust. Name what knocked you down. Give yourself permission to feel it, not fake it.

2. *Remember, You've Gotten Up Before*
   This isn't your first fall, and it won't be your last. But you've stood before. You've survived nights you thought you couldn't. That same strength is still in you. Make a list of past trials you've overcome. Let those moments remind you that this won't be the end either.

3. *Lean into Grace, Not Grit*
   Sometimes we think perseverance means pushing through alone. But the deeper truth is this: We get up not just by strength but by grace.

4. *Take One Small Step*
   You don't have to climb the whole mountain today. Just move an inch. Make one small decision. That's how we rise, one step at a time. Choose one thing today—shower, walk, pray, write, call someone. Let that be your first step.

5. *Speak to Yourself Like Someone You Love*
   You'd never shame a friend who's struggling, so don't do it to yourself. Your inner voice matters, especially when you're down. Let it be kind, honest, and full of hope. Write a note to yourself like you would to someone you deeply care about. Read it every morning until you believe it.

6. *Embrace the Beauty in the Battle*
   Life is incredibly hard, but it's also breathtaking. Some of the most meaningful growth comes not from comfort but from choosing to rise again and again. Start looking for beauty in the mess. Keep a light journal of small things that give you hope. A kind word, a moment of peace, a sunrise, a verse.

You are not defined by your losses. You are defined by your response. Choosing to get up is an act of hope. Choosing to keep moving forward is a declaration of joy. You don't wait for life to get easier. You get up now—raw, hurting, uncertain—and trust that joy will meet you in the climb. You have everything you need to get up today, not because it's easy but because hope is real, and joy is worth fighting for.

Chapter 11

NOW WHAT?

To live an Unshaken life means walking through seasons of uncertainty without letting them derail your identity. It means holding onto your purpose with both hands, even when the world gives you every reason to let go. And it means believing, even in the silence, that what you're doing and who you're becoming are not in vain.

It's not sitting back doing nothing and hoping that life magically unfolds. Patience is active endurance. It is the daily decision to continue, to remain committed, and to show up fully even when the outcome isn't clear. When you pursue goals worth having like building a family, starting a business, living out your calling, there will be resistance. There will be suffering. There will be setbacks. But resilience says to keep going anyway.

The goals that matter most aren't achieved quickly because they don't just demand effort; they demand transformation. A goal is rarely just about the result. It's about the kind of person it requires you to become in the process. And that transformation happens in the waiting.

Living Unshaken shows you that you are not what you produce. You are not the job title, the salary, the status, or the applause. You are the one who endures, who grows, who refuses

> *The goals that matter most aren't achieved quickly because they don't just demand effort; they demand transformation.*

to give up when everything in you wants to. You are the one who wakes up again, prays again, loves again, and chooses to believe that the delay is not the end of the story.

This internal shift—this clarity about who you are even when the world hasn't yet caught up—is what makes you Unshaken. You stop being defined by timelines and expectations. You become grounded in faith, values, and a deeper sense of purpose that no storm can steal from you.

Is there joy in the waiting? Yes, because joy is not circumstantial. It's not tied to the finished goal or the final destination. Joy is found in the growth that's happening beneath the surface in the quiet conviction that this moment matters, even if it's not the one you imagined.

It means choosing hope when things seem hopeless. It means loving yourself when life feels like rejection. It means showing up every day with courage, faith, and expectancy because you know your story is still being written. And when you remain Unshaken in the wait, you're being shaped into someone who can withstand anything and rise above everything. So don't rush it. Let patience and perseverance do their work. And what's the version of you that's on the other side? You'll be proud of who you became while you waited, while you endured.

Life is a journey filled with trials, setbacks, victories, and waiting. It will break you open and build you back again. But in every season, one thing remains constant for those who choose to anchor themselves in something deeper than their circumstances. Joy is possible, regardless.

This book and the movement behind it are rooted in that belief. Become Unshaken exists not to sell a lifestyle but to remind you of the truth that can sustain you. It's to remind you that no matter what you face, no matter what has come against you, and no matter how broken your world may feel at times, you are not defined by the storm. You are defined by the values, vision, and voice you carry through it.

As we reflect on the heart of Unshaken, it becomes clear that these principles are more than isolated steps. They are interconnected threads that weave a resilient and purpose-filled life. We began by *starting in silence*, carving out sacred moments of stillness to truly discover and understand ourselves at the soul level, not just on the surface. From there, we moved to *defining our purpose*, clarifying the *why* that fuels our journey and keeps us steadfast through every storm. Finally, we anchor to *building our lives on Unshaken Values*, grounding ourselves in diligent work ethic, discipline, patience, and unwavering resilience.

Together, these three pillars form a strong foundation, but a foundation alone is not enough. It must support a structure that grows and endures. Now that you've embraced these principles, it's time to focus on how to live them out with unwavering commitment. That is where true transformation begins, where beliefs become actions and ideals shape reality.

In the next section, we will shift from understanding to doing. You'll learn practical strategies for living without regrets, boldly moving forward even when mistakes happen, and ensuring your voice, rooted in truth and faith, rises above the noise of the world. This is your invitation to take all you've learned and build a life that is not only Unshaken but also vibrant with hope, joy, and the unshakable assurance that present circumstances are not your final destination. That hope and joy can and will be with you every step of the way.

No Regrets: The Truth About Living Forward

Living with no regrets has become a cultural mantra—short, bold, and empowering. But left unchecked, it can lead us to believe that reflection is weakness or that accountability is optional. At Become Unshaken, the idea of no regrets isn't about dismissing the past. It's about owning it fully, learning from it intentionally, and refusing to let it define your future. It's not about perfection; it's about progression. A life with

> *At Become Unshaken, the idea of no regrets isn't about dismissing the past. It's about owning it fully, learning from it intentionally, and refusing to let it define your future.*

no regrets doesn't mean we've done everything right. It means we've made peace with our missteps and extracted the lessons buried inside them.

Moments and results that you may define as failures or less than optimal are not burdens when you understand them properly. They are tools. They sharpen your awareness, help you evolve, and challenge you to take personal inventory. To live with no regrets does not mean you claim all your decisions were good or justified. It means you choose not to remain trapped in the emotional aftermath of those decisions. You allow yourself to feel the impact, and then you choose forward motion. Real growth begins when you stop using "no regrets" as an excuse to avoid responsibility and start using it as a framework for honest, hopeful reflection.

A common misconception is that living with no regrets means never looking back. But reflection is vital. What we don't process, we repeat. And sometimes that repetition comes with high costs, not just personally but professionally. Recently in my business career, I learned that the hard way. As my portfolio of Subway restaurants grew, I expanded rapidly—aggressively, even—believing that the same in-person leadership style and operational intensity I used with three stores could scale to twelve and eventually twenty-five. I was wrong. I didn't have enough experienced upper management in place, and I hadn't built a replicable structure. As a result, I found myself acting as CEO, marketer, regional manager, and sandwich artist every day in every crisis. I was drowning. I had no time for regret, but that didn't mean I didn't take responsibility. I had to face the reality that my original strategy wasn't scalable, and then I had to adapt.

What followed was one of the hardest, most humbling stretches of my professional life. I had to let go of control in areas I had never previously trusted anyone else with. I had to create systems, hire differently, delegate boldly, and build a leadership pipeline from the ground up. That season taught me to see failure not as a dead end but as a brutal but effective teacher.

The mistakes were real. The consequences were personal. But the growth—the wisdom that came from facing the storm head on—is what allowed me to become a stronger leader and ultimately a better man.

The truth is that "no regrets" isn't a hall pass for recklessness. It's a mindset for intentional living. We still own our words. We still acknowledge the effects of our actions. But we don't let the guilt of yesterday write the script for tomorrow. That applies just as much to relationships and personal moments as it does to business. Whether it's a conversation we mishandled or a strategy that failed under pressure, we choose to reflect without drowning in shame. We ask better questions, we get better answers, and then we move.

At the heart of a no-regrets life is the understanding that accountability and freedom are not opposites. They are companions. The more honesty we face our past with, the more authentically we can shape our future. It's not about living without mistakes; it's about living without denial. It's about doing the work to repair what we can and learning from what we can't. It's about trading avoidance for courage and blame for insight. And from that foundation, we move forward not in fear, but in strength.

Hope and joy don't appear once everything is fixed. They appear when we decide to walk forward with our eyes open, our hearts engaged, and our minds clear. Living with no regrets isn't about being unscathed; it's about being Unshaken. When we own our story fully, both the missteps and the milestones, we give ourselves the freedom to become someone stronger, wiser, and more grounded than we were before.

I've made my fair share of decisions that at first glance might seem questionable. Choices that others might judge as unwise or even label as failures. There were moments when the outcomes didn't look pretty, leaving one path for another, jumping into opportunities that didn't pan out, or investing my heart where it eventually broke. But here's the truth: I wouldn't change a single one of those decisions. Each step and each stumble has brought me right here to this very moment. If I'd chosen a different college, passed on moving to North Carolina when I didn't become a Chicago cop, dived deep into some music dream, or never married my first wife, the good and beautiful things I treasure now would be missing. Even the painful, difficult chapters are woven into the fabric of blessings I hold dear.

I often wonder that if my parents had stayed together, would I be the father and husband I am today? If life had been smooth, would I have left Chicago or fought for my current life, profession, and family with such desperation and depth? Every hardship has been a turning point, every loss a lesson, and every setback a setup for something greater. I believe that even though I have the freedom to choose, my journey is guided by a greater purpose. Nothing is wasted. The past fades as soon as it passes, leaving us with the present moment and the promise of what's to come.

What I've learned is this: Both triumphs and failures have forged me into who I am. Tomorrow when I wake up and yes, inevitably make mistakes again, I won't be chained to regret. Instead, I'll rise, ready to respond better, love more deeply, and live more fully. Living with no regrets isn't a license for recklessness; it's a commitment to keep moving forward, shaped but not shackled by the past. It's the joy of knowing that nothing is wasted and that the hope that each new day holds a purpose, no matter what's behind us.

Nothing Is Truly Under Your Control – Well, Except That One Thing

I have never met a person who did not seek to have control over their lives. Not one. It may show up in different ways and our inherent and natural differences may cause our attempts at control to look different, but inevitably and regardless, the desire is there. We hope to control our day, for example, when we wake up and have an ideal way we would love for our day to unfold.

Or perhaps we wish we could control the people around us. Maybe we want our spouse to say a certain thing or do something for us. Maybe we are hoping our kid will make their own breakfast and remember to brush their teeth without a reminder. Maybe, just maybe, that less-than-favorite coworker will suddenly show up to work with their tasks complete and a smile on their face. Larger desires for control might be the progression we want our career to take. We imagine the pot of gold at the end of the rainbow. If we could only get our boyfriend or girlfriend to change certain behaviors before we introduce them to our family. The list goes on and on.

Yet here is the reality. Your spouse is just as busy and tired as you are. Your child has way more important things to worry about than making your morning easier. That coworker still hasn't experienced a life-changing event to force them to make a 180-degree turnaround, and your boyfriend or girlfriend is still mildly rude. That is life. There are a million things completely out of our control. We do not control whether we wake up tomorrow or if we get some unsuspecting, out-of-the-blue diagnosis. Everyone and everything is truly out of our control, and if that isn't apparent to you yet, I pray it becomes so. Our attempts at control lead us to disappointment. How often do we hold others accountable for not meeting the standards we have for them without their knowing? How often do we become frustrated with people based on their being exactly the same person they've been since you've known them? How many times do we get mad over a tiny thing because it's now the thirtieth thing today that was out of our control and didn't happen as we wanted?

Control is an illusion. It's an ideal that our fickle natures put in our hearts. It is there to always make us upset. We desire the impossible, and somehow we still continue to expect it. When it doesn't happen, we become frustrated, irritable, and hold others accountable for our displeasure. So stop! First, accept that you truly are not in control of any outcome or situation. Aliens could arrive on earth tomorrow, and you are no Will Smith or Jeff Goldblum. You can't stop it. You are not in control.

Now that we have that out of the way, I pose an opportunity to satisfy that inherent desire to control something. It is truly the only thing in your entire life that you can control. You are fully and completely in control of you. You are able to control the way you respond to everything in your life that is out of your control. So how do you intend to wield that control? Will you use it for good? Or will you allow the negative feelings that are behind your lack of control to control your responses to them?

Every person seeks control in some form. Whether it's how a day unfolds, how loved ones behave, or how life's big events turn out, we all crave predictability. We picture smooth mornings, supportive coworkers, and thriving relationships. But here's the reality check: Life rarely obliges. People disappoint. Plans unravel. Circumstances shift in ways we cannot foresee.

Control is a mirage that leaves us frustrated and disheartened. The more tightly we grip, the more we are let down. And yet there is deep hope in recognizing the truth that while we cannot control the world around us, we have full authority over our own responses. That is where real power lies.

Here are some practical steps to embrace that truth.

1. *Acknowledge Reality:* Begin each day with a posture of humility and accept that you are not in control of outcomes, only your reactions.
2. *Pause and Breathe:* When frustration arises, take a moment to breathe deeply. Create space between the event and your response.
3. *Choose Your Response:* Ask yourself, "What response aligns with my faith, my values, and my commitment to joy?" Then act on that choice.
4. *Release Others:* Let people be who they are, not who you wish they'd be. That frees you from the exhausting cycle of unmet expectations.

This is not easy work. But remember, your ability to choose your response is your gift, your power, and your path to peace. As you practice these steps, hope becomes your steady companion, and joy wells up even when life is messy and hard. This is the heart of resilience, the art of rising, the grace of letting go, and the deep, Unshaken peace of living fully despite the things you cannot control.

Live Confidently in Your True Self

Anyone who knows me knows that I am unapologetically me. My father lived as if embarrassment weren't a thing, and as a result, he put my brother and me in many predicaments that would make people squeamish. Trying on clothes at Walmart, for instance, never required a dressing room. My dad grabbed clothes off the shelf and simply told us to try them on. The walk to the changing room, it would appear, was too far. Want to eliminate the feeling of embarrassment? Drop trough in the aisles of a Walmart. Embarrassment conquered! Or take grocery shopping. My dad would do anything for a laugh, including barking like a dog down the aisles of the local Jewel-Osco. Joseph and I would cry with laughter at our father's audacity and the comedy that his silliness produced.

The mundane with him created some of our fondest memories. But what else it taught me was that the world did not end with silliness. The public did not shun him for his behavior. He could be himself and chose to do so every minute of every day. There was no shame or embarrassment in him for simply being who he was, a goofball full of joy and comedy. Dad's confidence showed me that I, too, could be myself no matter the audience or the situation. It taught me that the world didn't end when I made a mistake or did something silly and that I could laugh louder than anyone else in the room, cry at a movie, or blurt out the first thing that came to my mind when asked a question out of the blue.

We live in a world that tries, often loudly, to tell us who to be. Subtle messages and loud voices alike push us to fit molds, hide quirks, and sand down the unique edges that make us who we are. But here's the freeing truth: God made no mistakes when He created you. Every laugh-snort, every offbeat hobby, every favorite show that only you seem to love are all part of the tapestry of *you*. Regret, shame, and embarrassment are tools meant to shrink us, but confidence in who we are expands our joy and deepens our hope.

> *But here's the freeing truth: God made no mistakes when He created you.*

Let's be honest. It's easy to hide the parts of ourselves we think are weird or uncool. But why should we? Life is too short to apologize for the joy you find in the small things. Do you love that sci-fi show? Own it. Do you laugh so hard that you cry and snort? That's joy, pure and simple. Do you get excited about bird-watching or making spreadsheets for fun? That's beautiful. Confidence grows when we let ourselves be fully seen, quirks and all, without flinching. Remember: You were not made to blend in. You were made to shine as only you can.

So the challenge is this: Stop trying to be the version of yourself you think others want. Author Jay Shetty in his book *Think Like a Monk* quoted American sociologist Charles Horton Cooley's concept known as the "looking-glass self." Cooley wrote in 1902, "I am not what I think I am, and I am not what you think I am. I am what I think you think I am." That reflects the notion that our self-concept is shaped by how we perceive that others perceive us. We often act in ways that align with what we believe others expect of us rather than from our true selves.

I am here to tell you that *that* game is unwinnable. Instead, dive head first into the rich, vibrant person you were created to be. When you embrace your true self with boldness, you make space for joy to flourish and for hope to strengthen your core. Living unapologetically opens doors to authentic connections and allows your light to inspire others to do the same. Confidence, after all, is contagious, and when your voice is louder than theirs, you remind the world that joy comes from living Unshaken in who you are.

No Rearview Mirror Living

There is no time for rearview mirror thinking. Life, much like business, demands that we keep our eyes forward. Every choice we make, whether in our personal lives, careers, or relationships, shapes the path ahead, but not one of those decisions can be undone. As business owners, parents, friends, and leaders, we face countless decisions that carry weight. Some will bring success, and others may bring disappointment, but the key is realizing that lingering on what's already done is a trap that steals our energy and joy.

There have been pivotal moments on my journey as a business owner when I crafted what I believed were bulletproof strategies—well-thought-out plans aimed at driving growth and positioning our company for long-term success. One in particular stands out. I invested months into oversight and training strategies that would better aid a company that had gone from twenty-five employees to 225 in less than two years. We launched with high hopes, but the results were underwhelming. Despite the careful preparation, it simply didn't resonate the way I had anticipated. The needle hardly moved. In those moments, the temptation to dwell on the missteps was real, but in the world of business, there's no luxury for looking back too long. The urgency of ownership demands that we process, pivot, and push forward.

Living without a rearview mirror means refusing to let past disappointments shape our forward momentum. To be Unshaken is not to ignore failure; it's to absorb the lessons quickly, adapt with clarity, and pursue the next strategy with resilience and optimism. Every stumble adds to the wisdom that fuels future wins. There's a quiet joy in this relentless pursuit, not because it's easy but because each setback is a steppingstone, not a stop sign. In business and in life, hope lives in the next idea, and success is often born just beyond the edge of what didn't work.

It's easy to let past mistakes haunt us as we whisper doubts about our ability to move forward. But here's the truth: The past holds no power except the lessons it teaches. Each wrong turn and each failed attempt are invitations to adapt and grow. The confidence to press forward, even after a misstep, comes from knowing that no mistake is too great to disqualify us from a bright future. Our lives are not derailed by a poor choice or an unexpected setback. Hope and joy remain fully available when we refuse to let yesterday's failures define tomorrow's possibilities.

Living without a rearview mirror means we stop wasting time on regrets and start investing in what's next. It's about pivoting when needed, learning with humility, and tackling new challenges with faith and resilience. Every day holds the power of renewal, and every next step is an opportunity to write a new chapter. Stand tall, trust that you are being shaped for something good, and keep your focus forward because the best is still ahead, and you were made to meet it with confidence, hope, and joy.

Your Life Partner Matters

Choosing a life partner is one of the most profound decisions you will ever make, and it has a lasting impact on your journey toward joy and fulfillment. The person you choose to walk through life with will either build you up or tear you down. They will either help you become the best version of yourself or allow you to stagnate in your shortcomings. It is crucial to find someone who supports you, challenges you to grow, and makes you better.

This partnership should be rooted in love, respect, and shared values, creating a foundation that can weather life's storms. I have always stated the following and have learned that it could not be truer. In life, we are given almost every relationship we have, for better or for worse. We do not get to choose our parents, our siblings, or the rest of our family. In most professions, our coworkers are given to us, not selected by us. Even our children are gifts we are given, and they are not chosen. The choosing of our life partner is the only true relationship that is our choice. I've made mistakes in my choices in the past. I believed I could change them, or they believed they could change me. I would ignore what they showed me and only focus on what they said. Discrepancies between the two did not give me pause. I thought I was strong enough, smart enough, loving enough, and more than enough to overcome the differences that would turn out to be impossible to change or improve. I chose poorly. And please understand that this does not mean the differences that led to our inability to work out necessarily had anything to do with overall character flaws as people. It simply meant that there were unwise differences that we wrongly believed we could overcome.

The voice of your partner should amplify your own inner strength. When you're uncertain, they should be there to encourage you, affirm you, and offer perspective when your own voice falters. They should be a mirror of support, offering both constructive feedback and unwavering love. A life partner who helps you believe in your own abilities and pushes you to achieve your dreams is invaluable. They are the person whose voice you trust when life has shaken you so much that you can't see the correct path forward. And you must trust that the intentions behind their support, love, guidance, and help are pure. I can now speak to this from experience as I have been blessed to find and have a wife like Stephanie.

In the very first month of our relationship, Stephanie showed me exactly who she was, not just in words, but in actions. When my uncle suffered his heart attack, I found myself in his hospital room, heavy with grief and silence, waiting for the inevitable. I hadn't asked for company and hadn't even thought about what I needed, but Stephanie knew. She quietly left work early, drove straight to the hospital, and waited in the lobby without expectation or pressure. She didn't need to be seen. She just needed me to know I wasn't alone. She even brought a small bag with my favorite comfort snacks, things that wouldn't fix this unexpected tragedy but might give me a moment of calm or comfort in the chaos. She didn't rush in with advice or platitudes, or make anything in this moment about her. She simply made herself available, ready to be whatever I might need in a time when nothing felt certain or safe.

That moment told me more about her heart than any conversation ever could. In tragedy, her love became louder. Her patience, empathy, and presence grounded me when I felt like I was floating in grief. And that's what true partnership looks like—someone who steps into your hardest moments with gentleness, strength, and quiet resolve. It's someone who says, without needing to speak, "You're not alone." Stephanie has been that for me from the very beginning.

But it's not just about support from your partner. It's about creating an environment where both of you can thrive. When you're down, your partner should remind you of your worth. They should be the one to help you see beyond your failures, guiding you with patience and compassion. And when you succeed, they should celebrate you, just as they would celebrate their own achievements. Your partner's voice should be louder than the negative voices around you, especially your own self-doubt.

But just as we long to be supported, seen, and strengthened, we must also be willing to do the same. It is a reciprocal relationship, not a one-way flow of encouragement. At different points in life, the roles will shift. There will be seasons when your partner is the one carrying the weight of grief, stress, uncertainty, or exhaustion. And it is in those moments that your strength, presence, and intentional care will matter most. We cannot only be takers. We are called to be contributors, to love with the same depth we hope to receive, to show up with the same consistency, and to speak life with the same conviction.

Marriage—true partnership—is the most important team you'll ever be on. You don't win unless both of you win. You don't grow unless both of you are growing. And you don't weather storms unless both of you are willing to hold the umbrella for each other when the rain gets heavy. It's not always glamorous. Often it's in the quiet gestures such as listening when you're tired, showing up without being asked, or offering encouragement without waiting for the "right moment." These small acts build the kind of trust that holds strong under pressure.

Loving well means showing up, even when it's hard. It means carrying each other through seasons where the weight feels too much for one person alone. That's the beauty of real partnership, knowing that no matter what comes, you're never alone in it, and neither are they.

So please remember this truth: Stephanie and I wouldn't have been ready for this kind of relationship if we hadn't each taken the time to prepare ourselves first. The silence mattered. It gave us space to heal, reflect, and get honest about who we were and what we truly needed. It gave us room to define our goals, clarify our non-negotiables, and become healthy enough to show up with both strength and vulnerability. When two people do that work separately, they're far more equipped to thrive together.

When it comes to a life choice, I don't believe there is a greater or more important decision anyone can make. Don't be like the tomb raider in *Indiana Jones and the Last Crusade* who reached for the golden cup, believing it was the true chalice. She chose poorly. Make the kind of choice that reflects wisdom, patience, and preparation because when you do, you don't just choose a partner; you choose a future worth building.

Your Tribe: Building a Support System

"You are the average of the five people you spend the most time with." —Jim Rohn

Just as you choose your partner wisely, you must also be intentional about the people you surround yourself with. Your "tribe"—the people you go to for advice, perspective, and support—should be people who lift you up, not tear you down. They should be people who genuinely want the best for you and are willing to invest in your growth. Your tribe isn't about surrounding yourself with yes people but rather those who challenge you, offer insights you might not see, and help you find clarity when you are overwhelmed by life's complexities.

Having a mentor, advisor, or coach in your life is essential. They are individuals who may have walked a similar path, who have wisdom to offer you, and who can provide guidance when needed. But it is also important to remember that your tribe should not consist of competitors. It's crucial to surround yourself with those who celebrate your success, and vice versa. They should be people who are secure in themselves and do not feel threatened by your progress. It's easy to get caught up in relationships that feel one-sided, where you are the only one growing or achieving. But a strong tribe is built on mutual respect and mutual growth. My tribe consists of only a handful of people, and on the surface they look like a rather diverse set of individuals. The common thread among all of us is that we build each other up. Period. Our hearts want the best for one another. And honesty with each other is a prerequisite. There are times when hard truths need to be spoken out loud, but the purpose is only ever out of support, love, and respect.

It's important to remember that you don't do life alone. No one does. The journey toward joy and fulfillment is meant to be shared, and the people in your life can either propel you forward or hold you back. Be selective in who you allow to speak into your life because their voices will shape your experience.

Another experience I have encountered with regard to adopting the Unshaken values is that some changes may be difficult for your original tribe to accept. Living Unshaken is different from the norm. In some instances and relationships, people may become uncomfortable with the changes if things like your faith, values, or priorities shift. And that is okay. As you begin to change, those who were in your tribe because you were mutually invested in each other's joy will remain. A true member of your tribe seeks to understand and help you achieve your goals, even if they are not interested in living or pursuing the same things. I would challenge you to do and be the same for them, always remembering that we are not here to judge others. Consuming yourself with frustrations over things you cannot change will only lead to frustration. Remember that there is only one thing you can control: your responses. Be hope and be joy, even in the uncertainty. Have patience as those around you begin to understand and accept where you are trying to go and that your aspirations are to live Unshaken.

The Thin Line Between Confidence and Arrogance

Confidence is a beautiful thing. It drives you to take risks, believe in your abilities, and tackle challenges that would otherwise be too daunting. Confidence is about trust. Trusting yourself, trusting your abilities, and trusting the process. But there is a fine line between confidence and arrogance, and it's important to walk that line carefully.

Arrogance is a trap. It's the belief that you are better than others, that the world revolves around you, and that everything you achieve is solely due to your own brilliance. Arrogance is rooted in insecurity. It makes decisions based on pride and ego, not wisdom and foresight. You might have the ambition to achieve great things, but if your motivation is rooted in the desire to prove yourself to others or make others feel small, then you are setting yourself up for failure. The success that comes from arrogance is short-lived. It's built on shifting sands, and the moment your pride is challenged, it will crumble.

In contrast, confidence is quiet strength. It's knowing your worth without needing to prove it to anyone else. Confidence allows you to take risks, make bold decisions, and continue pushing forward, even in the face of failure. But it's also about being grounded. It's about making decisions that align with your values and purpose, not simply to impress others or fulfill your own need for validation. Confidence does not judge others. Arrogance does. Living out your life and values with confidence should not lead you to point fingers at others who don't live in the same manner or with the same values as you do.

The Gospel of Matthew depicts this perfectly.

Why do you look at the speck of sawdust in your brother's eye and pay no attention to the plank in your own eye? How can you say to your brother, "Let me take the speck out of your eye," when all the time there is a plank in your own eye? You hypocrite, first take the plank out of your own eye, and then you will see clearly to remove the speck from your brother's eye.

—Matt. 7:3–5

This passage is part of Jesus's Sermon on the Mount that emphasizes humility, self-awareness, and avoiding hypocrisy in judgment. To be Unshaken isn't a call to arrogance. It is a call to joy, hope, and peace. Our goal is to be an example for and to others. The best way to help give these gifts to others is simply by being an approachable example, to live with and carry ourselves with such a light that others inquire and are intrigued. We are to stand confidently in who we are, not judgmental of others.

Stephanie and I were discussing the concept of embarrassment over dinner one evening, and she presented me with a hypothetical question. She asked me to imagine I was sitting courtside at a basketball game next to Michael Jordan, and I was chosen to shoot ten free throws in front of a crowded arena and, of course, the GOAT. She proceeded to ask that if I missed all ten, would I be embarrassed? She hardly got the question out before I responded, "I would never miss ten free throws." Is that confidence or arrogance? I believe that response is confidence, pure and simple. First, my assumption was that it would be impossible for me to miss all ten. I've dedicated much of my life to the game of basketball and still play pretty regularly. History would show that it is something I can still do at a fine level for a forty-something-year-old man. Does that mean it would truly be impossible for me to miss all ten shots? Not at all. I know it is a possibility, but my mindset is such that I would not allow that possibility to enter my mind. I drive positive outcomes with positive thoughts. I live, work, think, and compete with an Unshaken Mindset.

In the same breath, I proceeded to say, "Imagine I made all ten. Would I walk off that line thinking I was the best basketball player in the arena and in fact was so arrogant and proud that I'd challenge Michael Jordan to a game then and there?" Absolutely no chance. Arrogance breeds a sense of superiority and bravado that is unfounded, illogical, and often offensive to others. Confidence is a mindset that helps drive you toward positivity and hope internally.

When you approach life with confidence, you make decisions that are thoughtful, strategic, and meaningful. You don't overextend yourself just to feel important, and you don't work toward goals that are rooted in vanity. Instead, you ask yourself why you want to pursue something. Is it because it will bring lasting fulfillment? Or is it because it will provide temporary validation? True confidence comes from knowing your purpose and walking toward it with integrity.

So would I actually make all ten free throws? I can only hope for the opportunity to find out. But if my time on *Wheel of Fortune* is any indicator, I'd say I'm confident enough to give it my best shot.

Your Voice Is Your Power

When life gets noisy, it's easy to lose sight of your own voice. You might start listening to the opinions of others more than you listen to your own heart. You might find yourself swayed by the expectations of your partner, friends, or coworkers instead of tuning in to your own inner guidance. But your voice should be louder than theirs.

That doesn't mean you should ignore the wisdom of others or reject helpful feedback. It means that your voice—the one that comes from your core, from your deepest values—should always hold the most weight.

I have found that my voice has never been questioned more than in the realm of parenting, both directly from my children and also from friends, acquaintances, and the media. My Unshaken values reflect my commitment to parenting in ways that are firmly rooted in those values, not in trends or social pressures. I raise my children in ways that might seem countercultural, not because I enjoy swimming against the current but because I genuinely believe it's what's best for them.

When I walked my kids to the bus stop, it wasn't unusual to see elementary school children scrolling on smartphones, earbuds in, barely looking up to say hello or quietly whispering about what they were watching. And just last night, my thirteen-year-old presented his argument—again—for why he should have a phone of his own and why he should be allowed to stay up "as late as his friends" or "watch what they watch." But our family simply doesn't agree with that approach. Are we right? Are others wrong? That's not the point. I'm not interested in winning that debate. What matters is that I remain confident in the parenting decisions I make, not because they're popular but because they're intentional.

The same resolve that guides how I raise my children also guides how I lead in business. When someone suggests a shortcut around a hard process or proposes "playing the game" to win faster, I respectfully decline. If I'm not anchored in values, my voice risks being drowned out by louder opinions, the media, or the never-ending barrage of external influence. But I've learned that your voice is your power, and if you don't protect it, it gets lost. Whether I'm parenting my kids, running a company, or standing firm in the face of opposing ideas, my goal is the same—to live and lead Unshaken. That doesn't mean I'm inflexible or unwilling to learn. It means I've chosen to filter every decision through a lens of deeply held conviction, not fleeting consensus. There is peace in that, and more often than not, there is joy.

> *Whether I'm parenting my kids, running a company, or standing firm in the face of opposing ideas, my goal is the same—to live and lead Unshaken.*

You need to know who you are and what you stand for so when the voices around you get loud, your voice will remain steady, clear, and true. Your voice is your power. It's the tool that will carry you through every season of life and through every trial and triumph. But it's not just about your own voice. It's also about the voices you choose to amplify. If you surround yourself with voices that are negative, insecure, or cynical, their words will drown out your own. But if you choose to surround yourself with people who empower you, who speak life and truth into you, then your voice will only get stronger.

Trusting Your Voice

How do you make your voice louder than theirs? It starts with trusting yourself. It's trusting your intuition, your beliefs, and your purpose. It's about taking ownership of your decisions and not letting fear, doubt, or the opinions of others dictate your course.

It's also about learning to silence the negative voices in your head, the ones that say you're not good enough, you'll never succeed, or you're not worthy. Those voices are often the loudest, but they don't have to win. Through positive self-talk, prayer, therapy, and reflection, you can replace those negative thoughts with affirmations of truth and strength. Your voice should be one of encouragement, possibility, and hope.

> *Your voice should be one of encouragement, possibility, and hope.*

You are the one who controls your narrative. Your voice matters. And while the opinions of your partner, tribe, and the world around you are important, they should never drown out the sound of your own heart. Choose your voice. Make it louder than the negative voices, louder than the doubts, and louder than the expectations of others.

And when you choose to make your voice the loudest, when you choose to believe in yourself, you will create a life filled with hope, joy, and purpose. So let your voice be the one that carries you forward, that reminds you of your worth, and that pushes you to become the person you were meant to be. Don't let anyone silence you.

Chapter 12

A PERSONAL REFLECTION

I would be lying if I said that living Unshaken means you'll never feel shaken. We are human, and life throws curveballs that no amount of preparation can fully brace us for. And I have been through my own storms that left me gasping for breath, clinging to whatever thread of faith and strength I could find.

I think back to one of the most harrowing times in my life when one of my children fell seriously ill. We went through a season of endless doctor visits, tests, and inconclusive answers. The words no parent ever wants to hear were whispered around us. Cancer. Leukemia. I can still remember sitting in sterile hospital rooms awaiting test results, my mind racing, my heart breaking. I had no power to change the situation, no way to carry the weight of it on my own. In those moments, the only thing I could do was stay on my knees and pray desperately for strength because I didn't have it myself. The values and principles of living Unshaken that I share in this book hadn't yet become concrete in me. I was learning, but I was also breaking.

And that wasn't the only time. I've had other nights of deep fear and vulnerability, like the night when another one of my children required immediate emergency surgery. The hours waiting for updates felt endless, my heart pounding with dread. And there was the moment another one of my children endured a brutal experience during their birth where everything seemed to hang by a thread, and we feared for their life. These aren't just stories. They are part of the fabric of my life, moments that have marked me and reminded me of my own frailty.

Marcus Aurelius was a Roman emperor who ruled from AD 161–180 and is widely regarded as one of the most respected leaders in ancient history. Despite holding immense political and military power, he privately wrote *Meditations*, a philosophical diary exploring the emotional and ethical challenges of leadership and life. As a committed Stoic, he sought to live with integrity and clarity amid constant personal and political adversity. He was one of the most powerful men in the world, yet in his private journals, he often lamented the weight of life and the weariness of dealing with difficult people and inner battles. His honesty reminds us that no one is immune to frustration, not even an emperor.

He began each day preparing himself to face disappointment, betrayal, and ego, but he did so with grounded purpose. He believed that our power lies not in controlling the world but in mastering our response to it. His words are a reminder that the storm outside doesn't have to shake the peace within. In a time when we often measure worth by how "together" we appear, Marcus Aurelius invites us to lead with endurance and inner strength. Even in struggle he found meaning, and through meaning he found a kind of joy that no circumstance could steal. "When you wake up in the morning, tell yourself: the people I deal with today will be meddling, ungrateful, arrogant, dishonest, jealous and surly.... none of them can hurt me" (*Meditations*, Book 2). This shows not only the hardship of dealing with others but also the inner discipline required to endure with grace—a Stoic version of lamenting life's difficulties.

Christians, remember in the Garden of Gethsemane, we see Jesus, fully divine yet fully human, deeply shaken as He prays, "Father, if you are willing, take this cup from me; yet not my will, but yours be done" (Luke 22:42). In His agony, He expressed the weight of suffering so intensely that His sweat became like drops of blood. Later, on the cross, He cried out, "My God, my God, why have you forsaken me?" (Matt. 27:46). Those moments remind us that even Jesus in His humanity felt the full force of grief, fear, and abandonment.

In our own struggles, when we feel shaken by trials, we can take heart knowing we are not alone in those feelings. We have permission to lament and pour out our hearts in raw honesty, just as Jesus did. The Psalms are filled with cries of lament and questions of how long and why, showing that voicing our pain is not a sign of weak faith but part of a faithful journey.

Everyone acknowledges the inescapable pain of life, but my hope is that you learn that it can be transformed—not denied—through presence and awareness. These voices show that even the most disciplined and spiritually grounded individuals have acknowledged the heaviness of life. Their strength was not in avoiding hardship but in how they chose to face it.

> *Their strength was not in avoiding hardship but in how they chose to face it.*

What I want to emphasize is that being Unshaken does not mean being invincible. It does not mean we will never feel fear, heartbreak, or devastation. Living Unshaken doesn't grant us immunity from suffering. What it does give us is a foundation to stand on when everything around us feels like it's falling apart. It's a set of values, a mindset, or a framework that even when we are overwhelmed can keep us from collapsing entirely.

Those experiences taught me that perfection is not the goal. None of us will walk through this life without being knocked down or broken at some point. But living Unshaken means we commit to getting back up. We commit to holding fast to the values of discipline, work ethic, patience, and perseverance, even when our strength feels like it's gone.

So yes, I've been shaken. I've wept. I've doubted. But I've also seen how these principles—imperfectly lived out—have carried me through. They don't make life's pain disappear, but they offer a steady hand, a reminder of who I am, why I'm here, and what I believe in. And that's why my message to you remains one of hope and joy. It's not because life is easy but because even in its hardest moments, you can find a way to stand firm.

As we arrive at the end of this journey together, my deepest hope is that this book has given you more than just ideas. My hope is that it has given you tools, perspective, and most of all, encouragement. While the world around us will always shift and quake, we are not meant to be tossed and broken by those waves. We are meant to live anchored, steady, and Unshaken.

My Closing Hope for You

As we come to the end of *Become Unshaken: Joy, Regardless,* it's worth reflecting on one of the deepest truths of life—the constant tug-of-war between hope and doubt, between standing firm and being shaken. Underneath so much of what we face— the hardships, setbacks, griefs, and even the quiet moments of discouragement—there is a consistent undertone, the whisper of doubt. Doubt in the goodness of life. Doubt in our own strength, self-view, and ability to persevere. Doubt that seeks to keep us on shaky, unstable ground.

But the very tools and principles you've explored throughout these chapters were designed to help you confront and overcome that whisper. When you apply discipline, patience, perseverance, and the relentless practice of getting up— anchored in your purpose—you begin to root yourself in something stronger. You step onto solid ground, confident in who you are, in why you press forward, and in the deep values that guide your every step.

The road ahead will not be easy, but it is worthwhile. And it is one you were made for. Your journey is one of resilience, empowerment, and unwavering strength. This is the heart of Become Unshaken. An organization that believes in building lives that are grounded in joy, rooted in hope, and driven by the strength of conviction. Changing your life is a marathon, not a sprint, and with each step you grow stronger, more resilient, and more at peace.

> *Changing your life is a marathon, not a sprint, and with each step you grow stronger, more resilient, and more at peace.*

These aren't just ideas I conjured up. They are values first planted in me by my parents. Through their words, their work, and their example, they laid a foundation of strength and character that I am forever grateful for. But even with that foundation, those values don't solidify overnight. They don't magically become second nature. It takes time, sometimes a lifetime, for them to become woven into who you are and how you see the world. And the journey toward living them more fully and more deeply is never finished. That can feel like a double-edged sword. Yes, you gain wisdom, but you also realize that the opportunities to practice those values—often through trial and hardship—never really stop.

For me, nothing tests those values more than the pain of watching my children struggle or suffer. There's no pain like kid pain. As life progresses and the stakes grow higher, the trials my family and I face don't get easier. They get harder and more complex. Again and again, though, I can draw from the experiences I have had to give me hope for the future.

Remembering the early days of my business, there were times I genuinely didn't know if I would survive it. Money was tight. So tight that there were months I bounced checks and lay awake at night wondering if I was on the verge of losing everything I'd worked for. The fear was suffocating, and doubt crept in constantly. Was I cut out for this? Had I made a huge mistake? Was I on my own? And then came COVID, a time that piled trial upon trial. There was fear that the economy would collapse, that my business—the one I had sacrificed so much to build—would crumble. The stakes felt unbearably high.

Even more deeply personal was the pain of walking through divorce during that same period. Nothing prepares you for the heartache of family fracture, especially during an already tumultuous time. I was terrified of what separation would mean for my kids. Worried that not being with them every day would erode my relationship with them or my role as their father. The doubts were relentless: Am I failing them? Will they know how deeply I love them? Am I strong enough to hold steady for them when my own world feels like it's falling apart?

And through all of it, I wrestled with a spiritual fear just as fierce. The fear that all this hardship might pull me away from my faith rather than draw me closer to God. There were moments when I wondered if the weight of it all might cause me to drift, to grow distant from my faith and those closest to me. That's how doubt works. It comes at us from every angle—financial, relational, emotional, spiritual—whispering that we're not enough, that we're alone, that it's hopeless.

But in those moments, I return to what grounds me: silence, purpose, and a deliberate pullback to my core values. Even now I must consciously and continually fight against the enemy's greatest weapon: doubt. Every single day I remind myself that to live Unshaken is to stand in direct opposition to that doubt. It means remaining steadfast. It means knowing who you are and why you do what you do, and holding fast to the truth of your convictions even when circumstances tempt you to let go.

This struggle is as old as humanity itself. In the creation story in Genesis, we see the first seeds of doubt sown in Eden. The serpent didn't use brute force; he used a whisper. "Did God really say . . . ?" That whisper was enough to shake Eve's trust in God's goodness. Later in the wilderness, Satan approached Jesus with similar tactics, questioning His identity, His mission, and His trust in the Father. Those weren't just temptations of power or comfort; they were assaults designed to plant

> *And that is still how evil operates today: whispering, casting shadows over our purpose, our worth, and our faith.*

doubt. And that is still how evil operates today: whispering, casting shadows over our purpose, our worth, and our faith.

It's why we wrestle with questions like these: Why do bad things happen to good people? Why do we not receive what we feel we've earned? Why do we fear we're not good enough? These whispers of doubt are relentless. They aim to make us uncertain, unhappy, disheartened, insecure, and ultimately unmoored. Whether it's fear about the future, guilt from the past, or deep insecurities about our worth, the goal is always the same: to leave us unsteady, shaking in our faith and purpose.

But here's the truth. Every time you resist that whisper, every time you stand firm in who you are, why you're here, and the values you hold, you are living out the opposite of doubt. You are declaring to the world and to yourself that you are Unshaken. You will still face storms. Life will still bring pain. But joy is not the absence of hardship; it's the presence of hope and purpose in the midst of it. That's what this whole journey is about.

So take heart. The very existence of these battles means you have the opportunity to rise above them—to grow stronger, more resilient, more grounded. Every time you choose to get back up, remain disciplined, and work hard with patience and perseverance, you're doing more than just surviving. You're living out the opposite of doubt. And that, more than anything, is a source of deep joy and enduring hope.

Remember that living Unshaken is a choice. It's a mindset, a way of being, and a commitment to pursuing a life of joy, hope, and resilience. It's about aligning your actions with your values, embracing your purpose, and making decisions that lead you closer to your goals no matter the challenges you face along the way.

> *Remember that living Unshaken is a choice. It's a mindset, a way of being, and a commitment to pursuing a life of joy, hope, and resilience.*

Living the Unshaken lifestyle is not a destination but a continual process of becoming. When these principles and values become your foundation, you'll find that they transform how you see challenges, absorb others' hurtful decisions, and endure the unexpected trials of life. Joy and hope are always within reach when your life is built on an Unshaken foundation.

I wrote this book not just to share lessons but to walk alongside you, to encourage and equip you in your pursuit of a life marked by joy, regardless of circumstances. My hope is that these tools, stories, and principles will inspire you to live with strength, faith, and unwavering purpose. I believe in the power of a life lived with purpose, hope, and joy. And as you move forward, remember this: No matter what comes your way, you have everything within you to live a life that is Unshaken.

Stand tall. Choose joy. Embrace your journey. And know that no matter what the future holds, you are capable of facing it with unshakable strength.

As we part ways for now, my encouragement is this: Embrace the silence and know your true self. Anchor yourself in your *why*. Hold fast to the Unshaken Values. And when life shakes you, as it surely will, choose to get back up, again and again. There is deep joy and Unshakable hope waiting for you on the other side.

Be steadfast. Work hard. Be patient. Get up.

It is time for you to declare in both quiet and bold ways that you are Unshaken.

Epilogue
JOY, REGARDLESS

The storms of life are not a matter of if; they are a matter of when. Some arrive suddenly without warning, and others creep in quietly over time. I've lived through both. And while I cannot promise you that hardships will pass quickly, I can promise you that you are not powerless in the middle of them. You can anchor yourself to something deeper than circumstances. You can grow stronger while the winds rage. You can rise again, every time you fall.

My hope is that *Become Unshaken. Joy, Regardless* has given you not only encouragement but also the practical steps to live anchored, to endure with perseverance, and to reclaim joy even when it feels out of reach.

You are capable of more than you know. Not because life will get easier but because you can Become Unshaken.

RESOURCES FOR YOUR JOURNEY

The Become Unshaken mission doesn't end with these pages. It's a movement built to walk with you through life's challenges. Here are ways to continue your journey:

1. *Join the Become Unshaken Community*
   Connect with others who are pursuing an Unshaken life. Share stories, encouragement, and resources.
   ⊕ BecomeUnshaken.com
   Social Media Links HERE
   https:// https://www.instagram.com/become_unshaken
   https://www.tiktok.com/@become.unshaken
   https://www.facebook.com/become.unshaken/

2. *Listen to the Become Unshaken Podcast*
   Real stories, real struggles, and real strategies will help you live with joy, regardless.
   🎙 The Become Unshaken Podcast with Michael and Stephanie Rodriguez

3. *Coaching and Consulting*
   This is for individuals, leaders, and entrepreneurs seeking personal and professional breakthroughs. Michael Rodriguez brings decades of business acumen and experience, combined with his certificate in Executive Leadership Coaching from Harvard University.
   ⊕ BecomeUnshaken.com

4. *Events and Keynotes*
   Book Michael Rodriguez to speak at your next event.
   ⊕ BecomeUnshaken.com

ABOUT THE AUTHOR

Michael Rodriguez is the cofounder and CEO of *Become Unshaken*, an organization dedicated to teaching people, leaders, and organizations the *Unshaken Mindset* which inspires hope, joy, and perseverance despite life's hardships. His journey began not as an author or keynote speaker but as a husband, a father of six, and an entrepreneur who weathered seasons of deep challenges including financial loss, personal setbacks, and the long stretches of waiting between breakthroughs.

Born in Chicago and raised in the northwest suburbs, Michael graduated from the University of Illinois Urbana-Champaign. His professional path has taken him from social work to building a multi-unit restaurant enterprise of twenty-five Subway locations across North Carolina. Alongside his wife and cofounder, Stephanie, he has mentored at-risk youth, served in prison ministry, coached youth sports, and invested in building communities of perseverance and purpose.

Become Unshaken. Joy, Regardless was originally written for Michael's children. A legacy of lessons learned, values tested, and hope fought for. Today, that legacy has become a movement reaching thousands around the world.

Michael lives in North Carolina with his wife, Stephanie, and their six children. They continue to live out the principles of an Unshaken life—falling, rising, and repeating with joy, regardless.

SPECIAL THANKS

First, to my wife, Stephanie—my partner in life, my steady place in every storm, and my greatest encourager. Thank you for believing in this message as fiercely as I do, for walking beside me through every high and low, and for helping me live these words on a daily basis.

To our six amazing children—you are the laughter in my days, the hope in my heart, and the living reminder that joy is worth fighting for.

To Mom and Dad—your lives were the blueprint. You built the foundation, lived the example, and showed me that perseverance is not just taught; it is lived.

To my extended family, friends, and our Unshaken Tribe—thank you for your encouragement and support, for your willingness to band together in this mission, knowing that together, we rise.

And finally, to the One who never leaves, never changes, and never lets go—thank You for the storms that shaped me, the grace that carried me, and the joy that remains, regardless.

www.ingramcontent.com/pod-product-compliance
Lightning Source LLC
Chambersburg PA
CBHW070541090426
42735CB00013B/3041